Presented to

From

Date

Endorsements

In my most recent book published by Charisma House, *The Passover Prophecies: How God is Realigning Hearts and Nations in Crisis*, I wrote, "We must be a people of imagination like the early pioneers of nations. Isaiah 26 is wonderfully translated in the Passion Translation Bible. I love the way verse 3 is phrased: *those whose imaginations are consumed with you* (Isa. 26:3). The Hebrew word translated "imagination" is *yester*, meaning "form, concept, framework, imagination, mind". A human imagination wholly owned by the Holy Spirit is one of the most powerful redemptive forces on earth.

These times call for a critical, God-filled imagination. This will create a new framework and conceptualization of all the problems around us. Our minds should be fixed on and become consumed by Him. This is what will unleash the supernatural creativity resident in all of the redeemed and will give birth to the exploits necessary for our triumph. In this season, we must reform our minds and imaginations. We must gather raw materials, then shape them into form and identify our future. Our concepts, frameworks, minds and imaginations must unlock into new forms and identities to meet and triumph in the era ahead.

Dr. Barbie Breathitt's five book series, *IMAGINE*, has captured the essence of God's plans to reinvent the church in the fullness of Christ's creative, life-giving, resurrection power with signs and wonders following. Each individual believer must take on his or her Christlike identity as a Son of God to move forward into this era, as One New Man arises to demonstrate God's glory on earth as it is in heaven!

Dr. Chuck D. Pierce
President, Glory of Zion International Ministries
President, Global Spheres in Corinth, Texas

God's ways are higher than our ways, and yet we are invited to co-labor with Christ as partakers in His divine nature. Pioneering ideas in her new book series *IMAGINE*, will open you up to your limitless potential. You will come to know that God created you to navigate life with the mind of Christ, and by faith, you can tap into a Spirit-inspired, creative process that is aligned with God's heart.

Dr. Breathitt's books will help you to understand your call to walk in a prophetic relationship with Jesus and to unlock the powerful truths available to all who believe in Him. This is a fresh invitation to imagine with God, to dream with Him for the future and to access and implement heaven's answers to the world's problems to advance God's Kingdom.

Dr. Ché Ahn
Founder and President, Harvest International Ministry
Founding and Senior Pastor, HROCK Church, Pasadena, CA
International Chancellor, Wagner University
Founder, Ché Ahn Ministries

Many copy or imitate others. Some create a model for others to learn from, and some are innovative. But few are innovators. Others learn a subject matter, then reach a peak and just plain plateau and cease advancing. Then there are those who become constant learners as a lifestyle, filling their heart and soul with the creative realms of God. Dr. Barbie Breathitt is cut from this type of creative fabric.

As an educator and prophetic interpreter/analyst, this consecrated woman of God consistently takes us on an exciting journey of discovery. Can you imagine that? As you partake of Barbie's teachings and her adventurous spirit carved from the boundaries of the Word of God, you, too, will grow in your prophetic imagination into a place where dreams really do come true!

Dr. James W Goll
Founder, God Encounters Ministries and GOLL Ideation LLC
Life Language Communications Coach

Dr. Barbie L. Breathitt is on the cutting edge of using her God-appointed seer gifting to help people gain an enhanced understanding of how God created and operates through the imagination, so that His people can apprehend the mysteries and purposes of God and manifest His glory in the earthly realm."

Cindy Jacobs
Generals International, Dallas, Texas

Beautiful, wonderful and full of divine insight! *IMAGINE* provides the 'missing link' in Christian understanding and practice between the natural and the supernatural realms that many believers have been seeking for years. Dr. Barbie Breathitt has done the body of Christ a great service by providing a solid biblical foundation for understanding how the natural and spiritual interact—how we integrate that process into our own lives by cooperating with the Holy Spirit.

These books are both paradigm-changing and life-altering. It is a wonderful blend of contemplative and analytical biblical thinking, personal experience building and divine revelation that will provide earnest believers with a new blueprint for the kind of walk with God they have always yearned for.

I suggest you read these books slowly and thoughtfully, perhaps several times, because it redefines the normative Christian experience in many fundamental ways. As you train your senses (Hebrews 5:14) this way, you will find yourself thinking all things have become new for me now.

Joan Hunter
Author/Healing Evangelist
Host, TV Show *Miracles Happen*

Dr. Barbie Breathitt's book series *IMAGINE* is a timely message, as this is the hour that God is releasing creative thinking and solutions from heaven. These books will open doorways to anointed thinking and the ability to see in the Spirit. This will activate your ability to dream and create at new levels through the Holy Spirit. This series is grounded in sound biblical teaching and practical instructions of how to apply it to your daily life. It is not just for creative dreamers, seers or songwriters—it is applicable to all the gifts, especially in business and ministry.

Doug Addison
Doug Addison.com
Author, webcast *Hearing God Everyday*, podcast *Daily Prophetic Words*, and prophetic blog *Spirit Connection*

Perfect, absolute peace surrounds those whose imaginations are consumed with you (Isaiah 26:3 TPT). Our imagination enables us to envision the Invisible One and thereby, as Barbie wrote, '…to redesign the image of ourselves.' The imagination is uncharted territory for Christians. We need more people like Dr. Breathitt to lead the way.

Ron Campbell
DreamsDecoder.com

In her *IMAGINE* series, Dr. Barbie Breathitt's intensity of personae invites readers to partake in her deep insights, advanced levels of understanding and supernatural operations of faith in the glory realm. She challenges us not only to dream but also dares us to courageously imagine the impossible. Barbie creatively inspires us to unlock our potential in Christ through our imagination, to transcend the limitations of the flesh and progress in the limitless dimensions of God's glory.

I was often labeled as and teased about being a fantasizer during my childhood years, which greatly stifled the use of my imagination. The *IMAGINE* series has now unlocked the door to my imaginativeness, allowing me to freely and confidently advance. I have been awakened to the vast dimensions of God consciousness and His power, which equip me to exist and operate far beyond my God-given anointings and giftings. This series empowers me to live my future in the now!

Michael Adeyemi Adefarasin
Kingdom Lifeline Apostolic Ministries (KLAM), Abuja, Nigeria

A new era has dawned for God's people! A newfound season of supernatural revelation is being released from heaven to those who have the spiritual eyes and ears to see and hear what the Spirit is doing and saying (see Revelation 3:22).

Dr. Barbie Breathitt's *IMAGINE* series issues a clarion call for Believers to arise and supplant the old nature and attain their new identity in Christ. She implores readers to take on the very nature of Christ. She encourages them to utilize their divine imagination to create and decree their God-purposed destinies into reality in the same way God imagined and created before the beginning of time. Readers will discover the fundamental knowledge of how to apply their infinite imagination to shape their individual lives, influence the world and execute God's purposes.

Allow Barbie's *IMAGINE* series to transform your mind and usher you into a higher dimension of the Lord's destiny for your life!

Barbara Wentroble
President, International Breakthrough Ministries (IbM)
President, Breakthrough Business Leaders (BBL)
Author, Releasing the Voice of the Ekklesia; Becoming a Wealth Creator; Council Room of the Lord (series)

Works by the Author

Angels in God's Kingdom

Dream Encounters: Seeing Your Destiny
from God's Perspective

Gateway to the Seer Realm: Look Again
to See Beyond the Natural

So You Want to Change the World?

Hearing and Understanding the Voice of God

Dream Seer: Searching for the Face of the Invisible

Dream Interpreter

A to Z Dream Symbology Dictionary

Volume I Dream Symbols

Volume II Dream Symbols

Volume III Dream Symbols

Action Dream Symbols

When Will My Dreams Come True?

Dream Sexology

Sports & Recreation Dream Symbols

IMAGINE

EMERGING BEYOND THE LIMITATIONS

Dr. Barbie Breathitt

VOLUME 3

Breath of the Spirit Ministries, Inc.
P.O. Box 1356
Lake Dallas, Texas 75065
BarbieBreathitt.com
BarbieBreathittEnterprises.com
DreamsDecoder.com

ISBN-13: 978-1-942551-07-2

9 781942 551072

Published by: Barbie Breathitt Enterprises, Inc.

Printed in Canada.

Dedication

It is my deepest honor to dedicate my series of five *IMAGINE* books to my best friend, personal confidant and beautiful baby sister, Brenda Doreen Breathitt. She was born in Lakeland, Florida on October 29, 1966 and transitioned into Heaven on Saturday, September 7, 2019 at the age of fifty-two. Brenda was a brilliant light of joy with an excellent sense of humor that caused us all to laugh. Her warm, inviting smile disarmed people, letting them know she was a safe place to share their hearts. Brenda was clothed with grace, compassion and beauty that sprang up from a deep well within her loving heart. Her caring concern for others exuded from her countenance to bless all those who knew her. Brenda was full of godly strength and dignity.

Brenda's name meant *the glory of God's sword. Let all who seek You rejoice and be glad in You; and let those who love Your salvation say continually, let God be magnified* (Psalm 70:4). She laughed and loved well through her painful battle with cancer knowing in the days to come she had a home in heaven. Her thoughts and prayers were with her unsaved friends and family members that she was leaving behind. She spoke with wisdom and godly counsel always carrying faithful instruction on her tongue. She diligently watched over her family, friends and household never eating the bread of idleness. Her only daughter Chelsea arises to call her blessed. There are many women who do noble things, but Brenda's loving nature, quick wit, sterling character and integrity surpassed them all. We all know that charm is deceptive, and physical beauty is fleeting; but I praise Brenda for she was a woman who feared the Lord. Those who had the chance to know Brenda honor her memory for all that her hands have done. No matter where Brenda went she always found a friend. Her sweet words of comfort bring her praise from the city gates. Brenda blessed so many in her life with unconditional love, a listening ear, and words of encouragement, profound humor and a shared smile. Brenda made all of us better people for having known her. She is sorely missed.

Barbie

Thank You

A special thank you to heaven's Prophetic Poet Keat Wade for sharing the amazing poems he has authored in his four amazing books: *For Whom Beyond Beckons, Dueling Kingdoms: Chronicling the Times, A Gnarled Tree and Me,* and *Chronology of Love: Times and Seasons.* All of his incredible poems are available on Amazon.com and through Christian Publishing Xulon Press.

Keat Wade's poems are unique in three ways, (1) the supernatural way poems are received (2) the visual of what is going on in the supernatural realm (3) and being in sync with God's Timing (Hebrew Calendar). Keat Wade shares intimate conversations with the Almighty. He only writes what he hears. Keat hears or visually sees either the title or the first line. Nothing more comes until he starts to write. Then the words flow in poem form as a divine download, complete in one setting. Keat feels drawn into that supernatural realm until the words are complete. Then it lifts. The poems reflecting the Timing of God picture what God is doing in the supernatural realm, thus giving confirmation or direction.

Keat is a graduate of Fort Hays State University. He is a writer by desire and academically prepared with a Bachelor of Arts degree in English and Speech and a Master of Education degree in guidance and counseling. Keat retired from his teaching at Oklahoma Wesleyan University. Keat and Judy Garlow Wade now live in the San Diego area where his prophetic writing began.

Foreword

God is restoring our vision with provision.

Dr. Barbie Breathitt's *IMAGINE* series persuasively inspires Believers to embark on a journey of self-discovery, seeking and finding God and to discover His hidden, concealed mysteries through their sanctified imagination.

Readers will be immersed in God's truth and transformed by fresh revelation, soundly based on Scripture, crucial to this new season of operating in supernatural strength, powerful influence and Christ's authority. One is introduced to the aspects and mighty functions of the Holy Spirit, the Seven Spirits of God, God's communication conduits (dreams and visions) and how to use the awakened imagination to pray effectively, tap into unlimited favor and blessings, access healing and manifest miracles.

This is a new day of opportunity. Our divine imagination affords us the ability to know and receive all that God has destined for us to be and accomplish. It is time to increase and expand our borders. Barbie's writings challenge us to disconnect from the religious, legalistic ways of reasoning and exchange them for the creative, life-giving mind of Christ.

These volumes stir us to imagine the impossible, to consider how we think, what we believe and how we relate to God Almighty and others so that we can become Christlike, accurately discern God's plans and purposes and manifest His glory for His Kingdom advancement. Barbie has managed to successfully use applicable Scripture-based examples and captivating stories throughout the series to enlighten, encourage and guide us through a spiritual conversion of our identity that empowers us to apprehend our extraordinary future.

Our God-designed, ingenious imagination births visions of the unknown things of God and brings the invisible realms of creation into focus so it can become a reality in our lives. What we create and see in our imagination causes us to encounter and experience a broader dimension of God.

God's Spirit is advancing and positioning us through the use of our divine imagination to equip us with wisdom, revelation, fresh anointings and unlimited prosperity in order to draw the lost, sick and dying unto Christ.

Dr. John P. Kelly
Convener, International Coalition of Apostolic Leaders
InternationalCoalitionofApostolicLeaders.com

Contents

Introduction

This volume of the *IMAGINE* series expands on the previously learned concepts of Christ consciousness. You will learn the necessary skills to work with the Holy Spirit in the realm of the Spirit in order to receive spiritual vision. You will also gain the divine understanding that is necessary to fully transition and be transformed into your new identity in Christ. Volume III contains new revelation concerning the creative power of the words we speak forth, what truth we believe and how we see—all of the tangible and intangible things—through our God-designed, awakened imagination.

Every time we are resting in God's glorious presence (prayer), another veil is removed, so we can clearly see another dimension or aspect of His beauty. By seeing God in His perfection and splendor, we are transformed into that image of Him. *But we all, with unveiled face, beholding as in a mirror the glory of the Lord, are being transformed into the same image from glory to glory, just as by the Spirit of the Lord* (2 Corinthians 3:18).

By renewing our natural mind with the higher spiritual mind of Christ's thoughts and ways, we escape the limitations of carnal reasoning. In the day that God created man, He made him in the likeness of God (see Genesis 5:1). Man's fallen, carnal mind is consumed with a hateful hostility against God, but by utilizing the unlimited creative power found in salvation, our imagination can see God's beautiful face in righteousness so that we take on Christ's likeness. *As for me, I will see Your face in righteousness; I shall be satisfied when I awake in Your likeness* (Psalm 17:15).

If we obtain and retain a spiritually renewed mind that views life from

God's Word and heavenly viewpoint, seeing the end product from His creative perspectives, then nothing will be able to stop us from becoming and attaining all that God has planned for us. We continue to grow from one level of glory to the next. We increase into the next, higher plane of glorious existence when our eyes are focused upward and our imaginative heart sees and does what the Father is doing.

Visions and dreams reveal our highest calling, the answers we seek and God's directive plans and purposes for our life. They allow us to receive the spiritual understanding necessary to fulfill our grand destiny. Imaginative prayer brings into existence the things that have been concealed in the realms of the Spirit. Imaginative prayer also changes the confessions of our beliefs. We believe by faith what we are shown. When we can accurately see it, then we can speak what we believe, decreeing and prophesying it forth into existence, and we can seize upon and become it!

God is calling us to connect to and press into Him at a vaster, deeper level in order to receive all He has for us individually and collectively as the Bride of Christ.

Believers who have removed the veils from their faces see by the Spirit of the Lord with spiritual eyes of faith. Because they have submitted their whole being to the creative imagination of God, they contain and exude varying levels of the reflective glory of the Lord.

Jesus has the power to break us out of our current limitations. Transformation takes place when we die to self and transition into taking on the image of Christ. We must be conscientious and full of the God kind of faith to believe what the imagination is showing us. Imaginative faith assumes the conscious state of yielding to the feeling that we have already received the answer to our request.

The Kingdom of God is voice-activated! God is calling us to connect to and press into Him at a vaster, deeper level in order to receive all He has for us individually and collectively as the Bride of Christ. As we embark to identify what we genuinely believe, how to obtain and maintain clear, proper vision and how we think through our inspired imagination, we will receive fresh revelation to successfully advance in this new era as the Sons of God. God's mandate to us is for us to speak as He has spoken, to call forth those things that are not as if they were. This is only possible with the supernatural faith of God and the valid ability to imagine, believe, see and hear what the Father is speaking and doing.

Let Us Pray

Father, we come to You in the mighty name of Your beloved Son, Jesus. Just as Christ created the heavens and the earth, we are asking that His creative power is imparted to and released within each of us. Let the substance of our faith increase to activate our imagination so that our spirit can discover and apprehend Your ways and more knowledge of You. May we harmonize with the indwelling power of the Holy Spirit to help us understand how to frame our world with the living Word of God. We embrace the indwelling power of Jesus Christ, asking Him to arise in us to manifest His life-giving power through us. Amen.

CHAPTER ONE

Vessels of His Glory

When the mystery of Christ is revealed within us, our enlightened spiritual understanding causes God's miraculous glory realm to manifest in and through us on earth. By acknowledging our God-given destiny, the Holy Spirit empowers us to see beyond the present into the faith-filled now of the future. All spiritual understanding is gained by faith.

> *Now faith is the substance of things hoped for, the evidence of things not seen. By faith we understand that the worlds were framed by the Word of God, so that the things which are seen were not made of things which are visible* (Hebrews 11:1, 3).

Christ was crucified at the place of the skull, Golgotha, which represented His ability to overcome the limitations of the carnal mind of reasoning. At the moment of our salvation, Christ enters into our being. Christ no longer sleeps but awakes within the Believer's imagination. When we are crucified (cross-I-fied) in Christ—when we choose to die to self, fall to the ground and are buried, resting for three days—the old man disappears. When we roll the stone away, Christ ascends in us to resurrect us into our new identity. Salvation awakens one from the sleep of death to live eternally as a spiritually enlightened individual whose life is now formed and founded in Christ.

The Spirit of Christ dwelling within the Believer raises the soul from the dead to quicken the mortal body. *But if the Spirit of Him who raised Jesus from the dead dwells in you, He who raised Christ from the dead will also give life to your mortal bodies through His Spirit who dwells in you* (Romans 8:11). When the Spirit is quickened, the resurrection of the soul opens the door of entrance into eternal life.

Jesus is accessible. We should never look externally for Jesus' coming; He does not exist outside of the Believer. Jesus lives, moves and arises from within the heart (imagination) of the Believer. Allow me to paraphrase Matthew 24:23–24:

> If anyone says to you, "Look, the Christ in in the desert! He has returned to hold meetings at our home, a hotel conference room or this stadium or that," don't fall for it. If people report "He's in the country," or flag you down to say, "There is the Messiah!" do not believe it. The arrival of the Son of Man is not something we go out to see or observe with crowds. For the appearing of the Son of Man will burst forth with the brightness of lightning that comes to you, shining from the east, flashing across the entire sky to the west and illuminating the earth for His glory.
>
> But be aware that false christs will pop up; fake preachers and lying prophets will rise. Their impressive credentials, flashy performances and charismatic personalities will pull the wool over the eyes of those who should know better. These imposters will claim to be God's anointed by showing great signs and wonders. They will do these things to deceive and lead astray those God has chosen to be His—if possible, even the elect.
>
> See, I have told you. Be forewarned, knowing that I have prophesied it beforehand. Have you ever asked yourself, "How do vultures, as birds of prey, know where the dead body of a carcass is located?" They just know instinctively. And so you, as Believers in Christ Jesus, will also know when Christ appears, awakens and is resurrected in you. Whenever you see crowds gathering, think of carrion vultures circling overhead, hovering and ready to move in on a rotting carcass. Even though he is pulling in massive crowds, you can rest assured that the person claiming to be

christ is not the living Son of Man.

We are not to worry or be in fear. Having believed in God, we should also believe and trust in Jesus also. *It is expedient that I go back to heaven, for if I do not go, the Comforter* (Holy Spirit) *will not come and indwell the Believer* (John 16:7).

When an individual is born again into salvation, he or she becomes the house of God. The Anointed One moves into the body of the Believer.

> *For the sake of the name of our Lord Jesus Christ, we as brothers and sisters should agree to live in unity with one another by putting to rest any division that attempts to tear us apart. By living in perfect harmony, we are restored as one united body. When we learn to dance to the same music and share the same godly values, we will have taken hold of a common perspective* (1 Corinthians 1:10).

God sets up a living habitation within a human frame. We are each a vital part in the housings of the Holy Spirit, the Spirit of Christ, God the Father and the entire Kingdom of God. *Now you are the Body of Christ, and members individually* (1 Corinthians 12:27).

God wonderfully created our bodies to fully house the Kingdom of God and all of His omnipresent Spirit. *Neither shall they say, "See here!" or "See there!" The Kingdom of God is not discovered in one place or the other. For indeed, the Kingdom of God is expanding within you* (Luke 17:21). The more we discover about God, the more His eternal, enlarging Kingdom grows, escalates and intensifies in us. God indwells Believers in all of His majestic fullness.

> When the mystery of Christ is revealed within us, our enlightened spiritual understanding causes God's miraculous glory realm to manifest in and through us on earth.

Jesus taught us not to depend on the outward manifestation of seeing Jesus in bodily form. We are to trust in the nearer than here and the sooner than now presence of the indwelling Spirit of God within our body. *The Body of Christ is made up of many people all mingled and vitally joined together with one another, with each one contributing to the other as one body in Christ* (Romans 12:5).

We are born again from above, in and by the Spirit of God, when Jesus descends and comes into the Believer. *As the Body of Christ all of our individual bodies belong to Christ as His body parts* (1 Corinthians 6:15).

When Christ awoke within man, He united all of us with the power and wisdom of God. *Blessed be the God and Father of our Lord Jesus Christ, who according to His abundant mercy has given us new life, we are born again into a living energetic hope through the resurrection of Jesus Christ from the dead* (1 Peter 1:3).

The purpose of our individual lives joining with our brothers and sisters in Christ is to form a unified front to fulfill Scripture.

And if Christ is in you, He will live His life through you. The body is dead because of the effects of sin, but Christ's life-giving Spirit imparts His life to you. Your right standing in Christ causes you to be fully accepted in God (Romans 8:10).

Jesus was born to a virgin called Mary in a lowly, humble state. At His birth, He was housed in an animal's manger. Jesus walked the earth divested of His powers of divinity. As a man, Jesus was tempted in every way as any other man, yet He never sinned. Jesus, just like each one of us, had to look to a higher source of power, so He sought His heavenly Father for wisdom. Joseph only represented Jesus' earthly father; Jesus' real heavenly Father dwelt in heaven.

> *Salvation awakens one from the sleep of death to live eternally as a spiritually enlightened individual whose life is now founded in Christ.*

God the Father resided in a far greater dimension than the earthly realm that Jesus dwelt in for thirty-three years. In order to ascend into a higher state of being, Jesus had to focus His love, attention, times of meditation and prayer on scaling a heavenly ladder in order to be with or to be in one accord with His Father. Through peacefully focusing His love and attention on His Father, Jesus could hear, touch, feel and see what His Father was doing in another dimension. This is how Jesus was able to ascertain His heavenly Father's perfect will.

Out of the Imagination

Through the portal of time we came
Fulfilling destinies of many
For intercessory training and completion,
Securing nation's prophetic destiny.
As we exit, all Heaven is smiling
Hearing a hearty, deep-throated,
"Well done, good and faithful…
Wait, rest, and prepare; imagine with Me
Father of imagination, again…
Be strengthened in Me."

Keat Wade 02/08/20 (13 Sh'-vat 5780)

God the Father is the Creator and Ruler of All Things. He is the Provider and Granter of eternal salvation through Christ. Therefore, Believers should lean their entire human personality on God in absolute trust and confidence in His power, wisdom and goodness. The Messiah is always the same yesterday, today and forever throughout all the ages (see Hebrews 13:7–8).

Once Jesus knew the Father's will, He asked to gain an infusion of wisdom and power in so that He could accomplish His Father's will on earth. Scripture states, *Christ is the Power of God and the Wisdom of God* (1 Corinthians 1:24).

Whatever Jesus saw His Father doing in heaven, He obediently mirrored and displayed on earth. Jesus declared in a solemn oath to us:

> *The Son is able to do nothing of Himself, of His own wisdom, power or accord; but He is only able to do what He sees His Father doing, for whatever the Father does in Heaven is what the Son mirrors and does in the very same way on earth* (John 5:19).

Christ's diligence in seeking His Father gave Christ a 100 percent success rate. Jesus did nothing on His own. Jesus never functioned independently of His Father. Jesus Christ did not do things by His own independent design or in His own strength or power. Jesus accomplished more in three and a half years of ministry than most of us achieve in a lifetime.

> *Now to Him who can do so many awe-inspiring things by the action of His immeasurable power that is at work within us, is able to carry out His greater purpose and do superabundantly, far over and above all that we dare ask, think or imagine, infinitely beyond our highest prayers, desires, thought, hopes or dreams, according to the measure of His power we recognize and allow to work in and through us* (Ephesians 3:20).

In order to operate in any capacity as Jesus did, we must become like Him. We must believe, see, hear, think and act as Jesus did and does.

Let Us Pray

Dear Lord Jesus, we want to know You in spirit and in truth, becoming like You through our obedience learned through suffering for the sake of righteousness. We desire to have the mysteries of Christ revealed within us so that we are enlightened with spiritual understanding. We pray that the Holy Spirit will empower us to gain a glimpse beyond the present so that we can live in the faith-filled now of the future. We ask that the Christ who lives within us will awaken, move and arise to take His rightful place on the throne of our hearts.

Roll away the stones that have held us in a limited sphere of influence. Quicken us by the Holy Spirit so that Christ's resurrection power will open and flow through every door of entrance into eternal life. Our prayer is that the awakened Christ will unite all of us with the power and the wisdom of God. Our prayer is that we will believe God to infuse His wisdom, power and authority within the fiber of our beings so that we mirror and display His excellent greatness here on earth. Amen.

CHAPTER TWO

Spiritual Understanding

Our level of spiritual understanding is the truth of our personal story under which we stand; it determines the degree of accurate perception and clarity of vision we possess. People without spiritual understanding become fearful because their future is left concealed in the darkness of doubt and shrouded in unbelief. Without the enlightened leading of the Holy Spirit, they remain blind to every possibility that is positioned right in front of them. So often, the answer is right under our nose. Each of us is a speaking spirit who has the ability to open our mouth to prophesy, decree and declare into reality the amazing things that we have only imagined coming true in our life.

Discovering and agreeing with our true purpose and destiny will cause the displacement of some of our current, limiting beliefs and self-sabotaging actions. To obtain a higher, better future, we must repent for falling short of the glory. God has so abundantly invested in each one of us. If we do not obtain to our excellent greatness (by not being all we were created to be), we fall incredibly short of our potential.

To obtain the glory of our destiny, we must be determined to embrace Christ's higher thoughts, and we must be committed to making all necessary changes, not just minor ones. You may need to continue your education in order to begin a new career. You may need to move to a different city or state where new relationships await. Be assured that the results of the changes—the new, dynamic people you will encounter and the novel, innovative connections you will make—will bring forth advanced opportunities!

I have become familiar with having to make necessary changes, some quite difficult, in order to fulfill my destiny. For sixteen years, I was an elementary public school teacher. I was a part-time minister and supported myself financially by teaching children. On Thursdays each week, I would join Pastor Randy and Joy Bigger's Maximum Security Prison Ministry team to preach to and teach the prisoners who were serving life sentences in Florida. During the summers, I would travel with missionary teams all over the world. And on the side, I ministered twice monthly through my Breath of the Spirit Ministries training center.

I shut down my own ministry corporation in 2002 when John Paul Jackson asked me to move to New Hampshire to join his ministry as his Streams Institute Coordinator. I was responsible for recreating and developing his dreams and visions curriculums, as well as training his staff on how to interpret dreams. As John Paul's senior instructor for several years, I traveled around the world and trained people from every walk of life. I developed all of his courses and partner base, invented spiritual activations for the students, wrote articles for AWE magazine and served him faithfully for years. The skills I had acquired as a master teacher in the public school system were used in the ministry to rewrite and teach the Art of Hearing God and Dreams and Visions workshops.

We are speaking spirits that have the ability to open our mouths to prophesy, decree and declare into reality the amazing things that we have only imagined coming true in our lives.

Right before I moved to New Hampshire, my dearly beloved father had died of autoimmune hemolytic anemia. The pursuit of my destiny required me to move from Florida's sunny, warm climate to a very cold, snowy New Hampshire, where I only knew one person. The first year I was there, we received twenty-four inches of snow. I had to learn how to drive on roads spotted with black ice and laden with snow drifts. I had to learn how to book plane flights, rent cars, reserve hotels for conferences and navigate my new surroundings.

I left everything familiar and comfortable for the sake of the gospel. I changed careers, left my friends and family to make new ones, sold my lake house that I had personally designed and moved into a small, upstairs, old garage apartment.

The changes I had to make molded me into the person I am today. After a period of time in New Hampshire, John Paul moved me to Texas to open a Streams training center for him. I still reside in the great state of Texas, working for God in my own 501c3, Breath of the Spirit Ministries, Inc. d.b.a. Barbie Breathitt Ministries and *DreamsDecoder.com*.

Believers can foresee the future through the eyes of God's revelation knowledge, so nothing can blindside them. This is especially true if we trust that problems or difficulties come to prepare us in order that we may increase in wisdom to ensure we continually grow and prosper.

We empower whatever we place our focus or our attention on. To dissolve a problem, all we have to do is turn our devotion away from it (the problem) and, instead, magnify the Lord. God gives us the wisdom that is necessary to become the answer to the problem. When we realize that we already are what we are seeking and claim that we (IAM) are able to do All Things through Christ who strengthens us, we (IAM) are able to solve any predicament with His great power.

Part of being spiritually awakened into the new birth in Christ is learning that not only does the fullness of the ever-expanding Kingdom of God dwell within the Believer but also so does God Almighty Himself. This knowledge enables us to recognize that we have continual access to the mind of Christ and the power of God. Believers have the ability to experience all of God and His glory. We were created to worship, enjoy and fellowship with God while ruling His grand creation.

> *Discovering and agreeing with our true purpose and destiny will cause the displacement of some of our current, limiting beliefs and self-sabotaging actions.*

An infinite wealth of creative possibilities—art, music, inventions, newly designed building structures, resources of untold wisdom and treasuries of riches beyond our wildest beliefs—are resident within the dreams of our visionary imagination. The unknown is just waiting to be seen, extracted and displayed by those who believe. We receive from the Holy Spirit when we enter into God's spiritual rest.

> *For those of us who believe, faith activates the promise and we experience the realm of confident rest! For He has said, "I was grieved with them and made a solemn oath, 'They will never enter into the calming rest of my Spirit.'" God's works have all been completed from the foundation of the world* (Hebrews 4:3).

When we recognize the presence of Christ indwelling us, we are able to focus on every one of His various comings and goings. Once we identify the ways and movements of God, we become consciously aware of these same powerful expressions existing within us.

Let Us Pray

Father, we ask in the mighty name of Jesus that You empower us to increase our spiritual understanding so that we can clearly perceive things by the Holy Spirit. Clothe us with strength and dignity so that we can laugh without fear of the future (see Proverbs 31:25). Open our eyes to see the hidden things of the Spirit. Position us to prosper as we agree with the purposes and destiny that You created for us to obtain. Sharpen us so that we are awakened to recognize the presence of Christ indwelling us. Guide and direct us by Your loving hands. Give us Your wisdom so that we can hit the mark of the high calling of God. Let us perceive Your movements by Holy Spirit, for we do not want to fall short of the measure of glory You have allotted to us. Amen.

CHAPTER THREE

Imaginative Desire

The concepts of Christ we hold as truth about ourself will determine our present measure of success or failure. We can easily accomplish the greatest feats in life by reshaping our imagination to match God's desired images and grand impressions that Christ projects to us. The visions that Christ gives us enable us to desire, believe in and see a variety of different possibilities. We can choose to establish a broader, higher, more prosperous life and future destiny.

The loving God we serve is the one and only omnipresent, omniscient, all-powerful God of universal consciousness. God is the gracious giver of His Son, the Author and Finisher of our salvation. Jesus is the Healer, Deliverer and glorious Light of the World. By receiving God's only Son as our Lord and Savior, we become Christlike. We literally take on and diligently embody all He is.

True worship is not a matter of being connected to the right church or organization. Worship is manifested in us by our having a pure, open heart of adoration toward God. Worshiping God in spirit and truth causes us to rise into a higher mansion by developing a better concept of ourself. We ascend into another mansion because we are transformed every time we enter into the creative presence of God.

> *Never doubt God's mighty power to work in you and accomplish all this. He will achieve infinitely more than your greatest*

> *request, your most unbelievable dream, and exceed your wildest imagination! He will outdo them all, for His miraculous power constantly energizes you* (Ephesians 3:20).

We must remember that God is limited to the amount of His resurrection power that we are consciously aware of working in our faith. Time and again, people turn back and tempt God, provoking the measure of the license of the Holy One of Israel to limit the Spirit's abilities to flow and intervene in their lives (see Psalm 78:41).

When we are consciously aware of the existence of a state of being—a way of life, someone's presence or the reality of something—all of these animated things become possible. They become possible if we lift up and decree the desire. We speak life to it, and it shall be established and come to pass.

It is an obvious conclusion that if we consistently dwell on our offenses, agonize about what we fear, brood over the people we dislike or hate or harbor unforgiveness, we will develop a root of bitter resentment that will continually defile us, rule over us and eventually destroy us. Bitter root judgments cause lack, weakness and poverty, and harmful bitter roots produce the fruits of failure, rejection, sickness and disease, which will continually grow and blossom. These dangerous, life-threatening attitudes carry much too high of a price to ever allow in, entertain or cultivate.

Bitter root judgments cause lack, weakness and poverty, and harmful bitter roots produce the fruits of failure, rejection, sickness and disease, which will continually grow and blossom.

If we sow negative thoughts of condemnation or judgment toward others, we will also reap the effects of those same critical downward spirals of rejection in our own life. It is critical that we learn to honor people and develop a kind spirit that enacts the Golden Rule. We draw blessings and increased prosperity into our lives by doing unto others what we desire for them to do toward us.

We have been given the power to choose life or death, happiness or sorrow, lack or abundance, cursing or blessing. It is vitally important to choose wisely at all times so that we will continue to prosper in all of our ways. The various conditions we experience in life are the results of our inner thoughts (the secret self-conversations) and the exercise of our free will (choices). We choose the type of ideas, desires or thought life we want to have.

The things we choose to believe about ourself should give us a determined hope that will empower us to make the right choices in life. The combination of these choices bids certain powers and people into our sphere of influence. The choices we make and the attitudes we exhibit (perceptions of others along with the concepts we form about them) ignites our imagination. The things we believe about ourself and others will form and shape, positively or negatively, events that will happen. It is the classic "shooting oneself in the foot" scenario.

> *Fear kills creativity; it limits and binds the imagination, which hinders our ability to try new things or move forward into the unknown.*

If we scheme to hurt or defraud others, we also rob ourselves of a prosperous future—health, wealth or other positive possibilities. I have witnessed the following schemes played out in my day, some personally: family canceling on an obligation at the last minute to cause a financial loss; destroying others' reputation by causing them to appear to be a person not of their word; cheating people out of their inheritance by removing their name from a deed; lying or gossiping about others; labeling others as greedy when they are generous; criticizing or belittling others.

The cords of restriction with which we bind others will also restrain our own advancement by closing or impeding doors of opportunity. The short restraining leash causes us to stall out and to be stagnant, and it will eventually choke the abundance of life out of us.

A scornful person is consumed with hate, and he is securely tethered by his own bitter thoughts, as destructive attitudes produce despair, more trouble and compound difficulties. The disdain that the individual spews toward others continues to manifest a heightened level of internal anguish. His loud distressing echo acts as a beacon of doom. The alarm radiates from his being. It signals misfortune to enter in, attracting pain, inviting calamity and even death. God scorns the scornful but gives grace and mercy to the humble. These poisonous, twisted thoughts and destructive actions release fear, which is one of the dreadful cords of restriction.

Fear paralyzes our physical, spiritual and emotional movements by strangling the breath out of us with its strict limitations. Once we open the door to fear, and it takes root, it will rule and reign every decision we make. It will strangle and destroy every relationship we have or will ever develop. Fear kills creativity; it limits and binds the imagination, which hinders our ability to try new things or move forward into the unknown. Fear imprisons us in the familiar until life becomes so boring and noneventful that we simply stop trying, hoping or expecting anything good to happen. Fear is a sin. Fear violently opposes faith, and it stops us from reaching our full potential.

We must take responsibility for our thought life, even though no one but God is able to read our mind. Sensitive people who have developed their spirit to discern will subconsciously react adversely to our critical inner speech. A condemning, critical, judgmental thought life will project negative images by releasing hateful vibrations. In turn, love has the opposite effect.

Love causes us to clearly see that there is only one body in Christ. There is only one race, the human race. We are all connected because the Spirit of Christ holds All Things together. We all have red blood coursing through our veins. Jesus is the head of one united body. The Body of Christ is made up of millions upon multiplied millions of Jesus Believers, all formed from the past, present and future.

In Christ, there is neither Greek nor Jew, bound nor free, male nor female, black nor white. The Believer in Christ is called to leave behind houses, lands, all other gods, mother, father, sisters and brothers to follow after the one and only true God. Christ is looking for an awakened, unified body of Believers upon which He can place His beautiful head. Christ's countenance is rising and shining upon a mature Bride, who intimately knows and loves her Groom. She now walks as a joint heir of Christ in the boldness of His glory. The Bride of Christ works unique, creative miracles that have never been seen before. Wonders and phenom-

> *Fear violently opposes faith, and it stops us from reaching our full potential.*

enal miracles are continually evident as an everyday event in the lives of Spirit-filled Believers.

As the Sons of God continue to be revealed to a world that has been calling for their manifestation, unprecedented exploits of power will be demonstrated. We renew the mind by applying the wisdom that is found in God's rhema Word. Love always hopes, thinks and wishes the best for others. Love never thinks evil about a person in order to validate the development of a malevolent scheme that would carry out a malicious or destructive plan.

We renew the mind by applying the wisdom that is found in God's Word.

Remember, no one has the power to provoke or irritate us unless we grant him or her that privilege. No one but you can make you think or respond in an inappropriate manner. People have a right to object to your opinions, beliefs and philosophies of life, and they are justified in having their own thoughts, desires and ways. It is okay to voice a difference of opinion or express an idea that disagrees, but it is not okay to become angry, hostile, violent or disagreeable.

Let Us Pray

Jesus, we come into Your presence with grateful hearts, for You are our salvation. Jesus, you are Healer, Deliverer and glorious Eternal Light. Teach us to worship You in the spirit of truth, for we desire to be set free to be all that You have created us to be in You. Show us how to honor You in all that we say and do. Remove fear from us, and resurrect our creative imagination so that we perceive the new things You are doing. As we continually move forward by Your unfailing grace, empower us to do unprecedented exploits of power to demonstrate Your love for the world. Amen.

CHAPTER FOUR

The Power of Words

No one can tame the tongue, for it boasts great things. It is a world of iniquity that defiles the whole body. The tongue, though it is a little member, has both the power to create life and to destroy it, setting on fire the course of our nature. For Believers to develop the ability to adhere to the instructions of God, to become like Him, we must first embrace God's love. God's laws, instructions, precepts and principles renovate us so that we can live our life according to the teachings and life-changing power of Christ Jesus.

I will begin with instances of when we speak on God's behalf. God lives and exists in the present-future tense of reality. For us to speak forth declarations like, "I will be healed, saved, delivered or changed," delays it happening by placing that action somewhere off in the farthest reaches of the future. By postponing things with our words, there is a dimensioning of the aperture through which the power of faith can flow.

To think, say or pray, "Lord, if it be Your will," is a statement of doubt and unbelief. The word *if* questions whether God really wants to do good, whether He desires to heal or whether He will supply all of our needs. It is far better to say, "Lord, I thank You that You have healed, restored and delivered me. Thank You, Lord, that You have already supplied all of my needs according to Your riches in glory." The words *thank you* acknowledge our gratitude for something that has already been done or received.

Let me remind you that God is NOW! He is the same and infinite IAM yesterday, today and forever! God changes not (see Hebrews 13:8)! God is eternally present, living in the now future present form of faith.

Let the weak say, "IAM strong, now!" Let the poor say, "IAM rich, now!" What we consent to believe mentally, and how we allow our emotions to respond to the circumstances of life, is the manifest reality that we will project to the world around us. A tiny spark can set on fire and destroy an entire forest range. A careless, wrongly placed or vile word can ruin the world, tarnish or destroy a sterling reputation and turn harmony into chaos (see James 3:6).

> *For Believers to develop the ability to adhere to the instructions of God, to become like Him, we must first embrace God's love.*

For things to be altered, received or changed in our life, we must move the request, statement or declarative action out of the past or future and into the present, sustainable NOW! If we persist in sustaining a positive, faith-filled projection of a new, life-giving reality, we will cause that pretense to manifest as a true fact in our waking life. Speaking about it or mentioning it to others has the same cause and effect.

Spoken words are alive and progressive. Words never disappear, fall to the ground or die. The words we speak enter the airways and then circulate and travel into the future. The positive, good measure of life-giving words we choose to speak (to ourself or to others) will confirm, bless, increase, prosper or multiply us.

If the creative words we speak are received, they will cause the receiver to flourish. If the gift of our goodly measured words of blessing is refused, its intended blessing will return to us. It will pour back into us and will be pressed down and shaken together, and it will run over. God will cause men to pour back into our bosom. The bold measure of benefits that we liberally heap upon others will be given back to us (see Luke 6:38). When we plant kindness, mercy and grace into others, we are, in reality, sowing increased blessings back into ourselves.

In contrast, negative and destructive words, critical words of grumbling, complaints or scandalous gossip that we spew about others will also confront, judge, shame, limit or bind us. Be aware, the words we voice are binding contracts to which we are held accountable. Our own words will condemn us for our destructive actions. *The foolishness of man subverts his way and ruins his affairs; then his heart is resentful and frets against the Lord* (Proverbs 19:3).

We must be aware that words also spoken in an effort to control others, or to cut down or belittle loved ones, will cause the receiver of those words to be in a state of dis-ease. We can easily be reckless with our words. Have you considered how adversely your negative speech affects those you hold dear, including yourself? You would be amazed at how negative internal propaganda shapes a false self-image!

To give you an idea of the power and potency of our words, Japanese Pseudoscientist Masaru Emoto conducted experiments on the effects words have on the molecular structure of water. His tests involved exposing water to various words, then freezing the water. When frozen, water that is free of impurities will form beautiful ice crystals. Water that is polluted will freeze without forming crystals. In one experiment, Emoto labeled pure water with negative phrases. After 24 hours, the frozen water that was once pure no longer crystallized into beautiful snowflake-like crystals; it generated disfigured, murky masses. If negative words can impact water so radically, imagine the effects they can have on people, given the fact that the human body is over 70 percent water.

> *Neither will a baby who plays next to a cobra's hole nor a toddler who sticks his hand into a nest of vipers suffer harm. All My holy mountain will be free of anything hurtful or destructive, for as the waters* (contained within Believers' bodies that are full of My glory) *fill and cover the sea, the entire earth will be filled with the knowledge of the glory of the Eternal* (Isaiah 11:9).

If scientific evidence is not enough to convince you of the profoundly injurious influences ungodly words have on the spirit, mind and body, just spend a short amount of time with a chronic complainer who uses all sorts of negative terms—you'll feel the effects! Moreover, if a person who is violated by evil speech is unable to freely express his or her emotions, the toxic feelings become trapped in that person's kidneys (the emotional center of the body, the house of our innermost being).

At no time should we speak discouraging or harmful words toward another person; for those hurtful words will lower our own frequency, allowing dis-ease to take root. Destructive words recycle back to hook, catch and ensnare us in our own spiteful trap, just like the evil Haman's plan to destroy the whole Jewish nation boomeranged back on him. Haman's deadly scheme caused his own death and that of his sons'. They all were hung on the gallows Haman had built to kill an honest, just Jewish man called Mordechai. We are warned:

> *Let all bitterness and indignation and wrath, passion, rage, bad temper and resentment, anger, animosity and quarreling, brawling, clamor, contention and slander, evil-speaking, abusive or blasphemous language, be banished from you, with all malice, spite, ill will, or baseness of any kind* (Ephesians 4:31).

If the immoral offenders of this despicable, degenerate speech do not cease their evil word cursing and repent, they sentence themselves under the very perverse critical judgement they issued to another. Consequently, they could find themselves alone, without a friend, divorced or widowed. No one can live in such a hostile, unsympathetic, intimidating environment of toxic control. Living with a constant barrage of critical, judgmental or violent words that penetrate a person's soul will eventually take root in the depths of their inner being, which will result in cancer or some other destructive disease.

Bone cancer is often the result of deadly, belittling words always being targeted at the same person day in and day out. People become sick when they do not experience success, even in the smallest of things. Sickness, depression or hopelessness usually occurs because someone is constantly putting them down. In response to the abuse, the body begins to shut down and function at a subpar level. The bones in the skeletal support structure begin to dry out, become brittle, crack and breakdown, which result in thin or arthritic bones, painful joints or crippling back pain.

> For things to be altered, received or changed in our lives, we must move the request, statement or declarative action out of the past or future and into the present, sustainable NOW!

Once I was visiting with a dear friend who was on her deathbed. She was dying from kidney cancer. The cancer had eaten away at her backbone, hips and femur. From her hospice bed, she cheerfully requested the ability to decorate the room in which she remained hostage. I was stunned when I overheard the caustic, critical, demeaning manner in which her husband responded to her. Instead of encouraging her to express her creative energy, he belittled and laughed at her. "Really! You want to decorate the room! You don't know how to decorate! You can't pick the right colors, material, textures or anything! You have never had good taste. You know you can't design anything. I am the one who does that. You don't know how to do anything right!"

When I heard the destructive words that came from his mouth, I knew why my friend was in the condition she was in. She had lived with his constant put-downs and criticism for years. Now her body was shutting down, unable to resist, fight back or stand against his hateful comments any longer. Her body was falling apart. He had finally destroyed her hope in a prosperous future.

The words we speak enter the airways and then circulate and travel into the future.

The words that roll off our tongue have the power to create life and healing miracles, or they have the power to kill by a slow, agonizing death. We choose the style of words that are either a curing, restorative salve or a confronting, demeaning declaration of destruction. In the same respect, it is wise to distance ourselves from those guilty of such negative behaviors, lest we twin their actions. *Do not resentfully envy and be jealous of an unscrupulous, grasping man, and choose none of his ways* (Proverbs 3:31).

Prophesying God's Words

As ambassadors of Christ, we are called to speak God's words. Speaking the life-giving, healing Word of God begins the process of drawing the kingdom of heaven to and up within us. A renewed mind that is focused on Christ will think higher thoughts. An ascended, God-focused mind will produce an energy that animates creative words. The words we choose to speak produce actions (positive or negative), and our actions create opportunities, which form a destiny. Speaking negatively in any fashion is speaking against God's truth.

When we are consciously aware of the existence of the things we desire, we have the agreement of two (awareness and desire) touching anything on earth; therefore, it will be done for us. Words are the seeds we gather, sow, arrange and plant to create the future harvest of fruits we will inherit. A word is a desire that is longed for, but it can only be manifested when the word is joined with God's conscious, creative power to become a reality. *In the beginning was the Word, and the Word was with God, and the Word was God* (John 1:1).

The prophet Samuel shared the last words of King David, who ruled righteously in the fear of the Lord. *The Spirit of the Lord spoke to me in my mind and by me, and His Word was in my tongue* (2 Samuel 23:2). The Word of God is so near to us that it is in our minds. It is imprinted on our hearts and dwelling within our mouths. This is so that we can meditate on it and imagine, believe and think like it, becoming the living Word in order to demonstrate it. The Word of God being near speaks of the slightest of distances. It indwells, overlaps, rescripts our soul, renews the mind, heals the body and gives the human spirit rebirth.

A word is a desire that is longed for, but it can only be manifested when the word is joined with God's conscious, creative power to become a reality.

The Word of God goes deep down within our bones so that the marrow contemplates the imaginative words we read, hear, believe, speak, pray, decree and prophesy! The Prophet Ezekiel prophesied, as God commanded him, to a valley full of dried, scattered bones. The dead, parched bones heard the thunderous sound of the inspired voice of heaven speaking through man. The dry bones responded to the inventive prophetic voice and came to attention; they shook, moved, aligned and connected. Strong sinew rejoined them; bones were knit together, flesh and skin covered. Prophesy revived them, restored life to them. The dried bones rose up as resurrected bodies. Prophesy formed a great army when the resuscitated (Ruach) breath of the Spirit of God took up resident in their soul (see Ezekiel 37:1-14).

When the dead man's body touched the buried bones of Elisha, the corpus was revived (lived again) and stood up (see 2 Kings 13:21).

Prophet Jeremiah said in his heart, *If I say, "I will not remember Him or speak His name anymore," then my heart* (imagination) *becomes* (enlightened and illuminated like) *a burning fire shut up in my bones. And I am weary of enduring and holding it in; I cannot endure it* (nor contain it any longer) (Jeremiah 20:9). When we receive with meekness the inborn Word that is able to save our soul, our inner speech and belief system is fused together, equally yoked and matched as one with God's.

The conscious exercise of our imagination empowers our desires to be seen and realized. When we receive, believe and declare the progressive Word of God, it causes the kingdom of heaven to manifest in our lives. When our imagination and inner speech fuses as one with God's words, the thoughts we have and the things we declare will be accumulated by us, for God has already established them. God commands the blessing to manifest when we dwell together with Him in unity. We must first be one with our own person and God before we can be whole and one with another person. The Apostle Paul wrote in Ephesians 1:16–20:

> *I do not cease to give thanks for you, making mention of you in my prayers: that the God of our Lord Jesus Christ, the Father of glory, may give to you the Spirit of Wisdom and Revelation in the knowledge of Him, the eyes of your understanding being enlightened; that you may know what is the hope of His calling, what are the riches of the glory of His inheritance in the saints, and what is the exceeding greatness of His power toward us who believe, according to the working of His mighty power, which He worked in Christ when He raised Him from the dead and seated Him at His right hand in the heavenly places.*

Let Us Pray

Lord Jesus, we ask that You create in us a clean heart that continually speaks forth Your words of love. Help us to place reins upon our tongues. Empower us to adhere to Your instructions and alter our speech patterns so that they produce life, healing and prosperity. We want to say only that which we hear You saying. Adjust our routine actions so that we reflect the power of Your words. Let Your grace be upon our mouths so that the words we speak do not fall to the ground but go forth to accomplish that which You desire. Amen.

CHAPTER FIVE

Empowered Prayer

The name Daniel means *God is my judge.* He was a Jewish captive who served as an advisor in the courts of the Babylonian king as the dream interpreter, a sage and wise man. He moved so powerfully in the dimensions of prayer that he fell asleep, rested on the pride of lions that could have easily ripped him apart and devoured every shred of him. Today, the lions would represent any overwhelming problems that eat up all your time, strength and energy.

Daniel was a gifted seer who understood the inventive resourcefulness of the imagination, the powerful art of prayer, the spiritual dimensions of mysterious dreams and artistic visions and the diverse realms of angels.

> *Then the angel Gabriel said to me, "Do not fear, Daniel, for from the first day that you set the heart of your imagination to understand, and humbled yourself before your God, your faith-filled words were heard in heaven; and I have come because of the power found in your prayerful words"* (Daniel 10:12).

Because of this spiritual understanding between prayer and the angelic realm, Daniel was skillful at interpreting dreams and divine secrets no one else could comprehend. Daniel's prayer life and silent meditations on God's truths and revelation elevated him to the highest level of prophetic seeing and oracular foretelling. Daniel's asking, seeking and continual knocking in prayer made him open and receptive to a higher level of spiritual God consciousness.

Daniel had purposed in his heart that he would be pure in his mind, body and spirit. He determined not to defile himself with the king's wine or delicacies. Daniel was given understanding of spiritual skills for governmental service. He and his Jewish companions possessed an elevated measure of supernatural wisdom and understanding in the mystical realms of God. None of the king's magicians' incantations, occult, evil-eyed seers or dark conjurers of enchantments could compare with their godly, sanctified imagination and divine spiritual skills.

> Daniel's prayer life and silent meditations on God's truths and revelation elevated him to the highest level of prophetic seeing.

God's heavenly wisdom does not consist of knowing concepts or even mastering spiritual things but of choosing to spend focused, quality time in God's loving presence in order to know Him and follow His perfect will.

Queens, kings and lords in the royal halls of castles called upon Daniel to interpret all manner of spiritual events and happenings.

> *The queen, because of the words of the king and his lords, came to the banquet hall. The queen spoke, saying, "O king, live forever! Do not let your thoughts trouble you, nor let your countenance change. There is a man in your kingdom in whom is the Spirit of the Holy God. And in the days of your father, light and understanding and wisdom, like the wisdom of the gods, were found in him; and King Nebuchadnezzar your father—your father the king—made him chief of the magicians, astrologers, Chaldeans, and soothsayers. Inasmuch as an excellent spirit, knowledge, understanding, interpreting dreams, solving riddles, and explaining enigmas were found in this Daniel"* (Daniel 5:10–12).

The kingdoms of God's light (understanding and wisdom) work on a gradient principle of change, increase and multiplication. *He replied, "I tell you that to everyone who has, more will be given, but as for the one who has nothing, even what they have will be taken away"* (Luke 19:26). Believers in Christ are enlightened, enhanced and transformed, and they are given more ruling power, authority and dominion according to the measure of faith and obedience that they activate.

Happy is the one who finds God's wisdom and gains His understanding; it causes him or her to seek truth. Good Sense will scout ahead to prevent danger. Acknowledging God in all of our ways ensures that Insight will keep an eye out so we are able to walk on the righteous paths of justice. Lady Wisdom will be our close friend, and Brother Knowledge will be our constant, pleasant companion. They will keep us from making an error, taking a false step or being led in the wrong direction. When God's wisdom enters the heart of our imagination, heavenly knowledge will be pleasant to our soul.

The measure of God's presence we receive is determined by the time we spend praying according to God's will.

Our prayer should always be, "Holy Spirit, create in me a clean heart and renew a right spirit within me so that the light of Your presence dawns brighter and brighter within my imagination and upon my countenance."

In Volume II, we learned how to practice the presence of God. The measure of God's presence we receive is determined by the time we spend praying according to God's will and higher plans, which transform and empower us to reach His higher purposes for our life.

> *This is the confidence we have in approaching God: that if we ask anything according to His will, He hears us. And if we know that He hears us—whatever we ask—we know that we have what we asked of Him* (1 John 5:14–15).

When the will of our mind is centered in Christ, we gain the understanding that is necessary to harmonize with God's higher ways. By synergizing our free will with God's spiritual understanding, we can stay focused on performing God's perfect will.

God created us as man, being both male (masculine) and female (feminine), in His own image and likeness as Sons of God (see Genesis 1:26). The spiritually born-again man has his or her being in Christ, identified collectively as both being a part of one corporate body and, at the same time, being uniquely individual. The divine man is Jehovah, the only Begotten of Elohim, Jesus, the IAM that IAM, the risen Christ. However, the weights of the world and the darkness of sin try to press us into a twisted mold of worldly conformity. *Therefore, let us, as many as are mature, have this mind; and if in anything you think otherwise, God will reveal even this to you* (Philippians 3:15).

Times of restful prayer give the Christ within us the ability to touch our heart and hold us in His loving embrace. Christ renews our mind and heals our brokenness. Jesus restores and recreates us when we spend time in His presence. *As a man thinks in his heart* (imagination), *so is he* (Proverbs 23:7).

Prayer empowers us to trust Christ Jesus with the keeping of our heart. *Keep your heart with all diligence, for out of it spring the issues of life* (Proverbs 4:23). Jesus overcame every issue of the heart and all that the world can offer. He resisted fulfilling the gratification of the flesh, the allure of worldly things and the pursuit for social status, influence and power. Christ found His pleasure in pleasing His Father, and we must too!

For no man knows his own heart; it takes the Holy Spirit to reveal and remove the deceit that is found there. *Every way of a man is right in his own eyes, but the Lord weighs the heart* (man's imagination) (Proverbs 21:2).

This life is a journey on which we embark in order to discover God. When we search out and encounter the depths of God, it is then that we realize all that we are destined to be in Christ. *Blessed is the man whose strength is in You; whose heart is set on pilgrimage* (Psalm 84:5). The Christ-conscious Sons of God find joy unspeakable that is full of glory that never passes away. Abundance is found in eternal life.

When we search out and encounter the depths of God, it is then that we realize all that we are destined to be in Christ.

The laws and statutes of God align our heart and mind, so we are able to follow Him on a pure path of love and light. *The statutes of the Lord are right, rejoicing the heart; the commandment of the Lord is pure, enlightening the eyes* (Psalm 19:8).

The people who live life with a pure, childlike and clean imaginative heart are blessed of the Lord, for they will see God. Every time our eyes see God in prayer, or we envision His light that shines upon our path, we are given clarity. Spiritual insights into God's revelation knowledge come so that we will never stumble or fall. *The law of his God is in his heart; none of his steps shall slide* (Psalm 37:31). We can be whatever we see in prayer if we believe and behold it with the childlike eyes of faith that are continually focused on trusting God, acknowledging Him in all of our ways.

To this day, we are aware of the universal agony and groaning of creation, waiting the emergence of the Sons of God, as if it were in the contractions of labor. All around us, we observe that God's creation is pregnant, so the difficult times of pain and suffering throughout the world are simply birth pangs. It's not only around us, but it's within us. The Spirit of God is arousing us from within, and as Sons of God, we are also feeling the birth pangs. These sterile, barren physical bodies of ours are yearning for full deliverance. That is why waiting does not diminish us any more than waiting nine months diminishes a pregnant mother.

Every time our eyes see God in prayer, or we envision His light that shines upon our path, we are given clarity.

We are enlarged with Christ in the waiting. We, of course, don't see what is enlarging us, but the longer we wait, the larger we become and the more joyful our expectancy (see Romans 8:22–25). Our spirit man grows and expands past our physical body, and it's radiant shadow of glory outshines God's presence to this dark world.

Let Us Pray

Holy Spirit, we ask that You teach us to pray in the Spirit so that we learn how to work with the holy angels to receive skill and understanding of dreams, visions and more revelation knowledge. Open our eyes so we can be gifted, imaginative seers. Help us to be pure in mind, body and spirit. Holy Spirit, create in us a clean heart, and renew a right spirit within us so that the light of Your presence dawns brighter and brighter on our countenance.

Thank you, God, that You have given us a confidence to know

that You hear us when we approach You, that You will give us anything we ask that is according to Your will. Keep our hearts stayed on You, for You, oh Lord, are the wellspring to our lives. Help us to overcome every temptation of the flesh so that we can walk in the power of Your Spirit. Teach us how to be like imaginative children so that we can inherit Your Kingdom as the Sons of God. Amen.

CHAPTER SIX

Connection to the Realms of the Spirit

We are told to pray without ceasing. It is our prayer life that connects us to the realms of God's Spirit. When we pray, we learn to seek, listen, knock, hear, ask, recognize and know the different sounds of the Three in One's voices. The Holy Spirit loves to reveal His secret, hidden things and show mysteries to us, provoking a longing to be in His presence and building an intimate face-to-face relationship.

The wisdom that God shares with us enables us to help people and leaders from every nation, tribe and diverse tongue around the world.

Let each of you look out not only for his own interests but also for the interests of others. Let this mind be in you which was also in Christ Jesus, who, being in the form of God, did not consider it robbery to be equal with God, but made Himself of no reputation, taking the form of a bond-servant, and coming in the likeness of men. *And being found in appearance as a man, He humbled Himself and became obedient to the point of death, even the death of the cross* (2 Philippians 2:4–8).

Heaven and earth bear witness to each other. The water of the womb of the Word of God mingles with the blood of Jesus Christ to form the river of Spirit and Truth. *This is He who came by water and blood—Jesus Christ; not only by water, but by water and blood. And it is the Spirit who bears witness, because the Spirit is truth* (John 1:5–6).

When Christ comes into our being at salvation, the spirit and soul come into agreement as one. The veil between the two is torn apart, allowing a free flow of the spirit to emerge and grow until it can rule over the soul. Believers are to be led by the Spirit of God, not by their soul or fleshly desires. This empowers justice and righteousness, as well as wisdom and truth, to reign in each of our lives now. As this divine coupling aligns, the subconscious and conscious also align and agree as one. *Again, I say to you that if two of you agree on earth concerning anything that they ask, it will be done for them by My Father in heaven* (Matthew 18:19).

Our regenerated spirit hears the Spirit of God. The wisdom, communion and consciousness of our spirit engage through the feelings of our blood-bought soul. When these two (spirit and soul) come into agreement, walking together in the faith of God and believing what the Spirit of Truth and God's divine wisdom are speaking, we are then able to hear, visualize and receive the answers to our prayers that have been waiting from the Genesis of creation on us to discover their existence.

When there is spiritual alignment, the gears and tumblers of the lock are arranged in a parallel fashion to allow the kingdom key to fit inside. When the kingdom key is activated or turned, the lock is opened. Each and every kingdom key gives the person access and ownership to whatever dimension, mansion, vehicle, property or safe deposit asset that lies behind the door.

Each and every kingdom key gives the person access and ownership to whatever dimension, mansion, vehicle, property or safe deposit asset lies behind the door.

The same is true of the Believer's life. When we align our heart with God in salvation, everything begins to fall into place. We are given the keys to the Kingdom of God. These keys give us access to Jesus (Eternal Door), who leads to the Father and all of His heavenly mansions. Jesus is the answer to every question and need. When we step into Jesus, we are given access to the Father and the Holy Spirit.

As joint heirs of Christ, we learn to seek God with all of our heart, soul and strength of our spirit until we are given entry into the kingdom of heaven, which is within. The Bible confirms: *If we will seek God with all of our heart,*

He will be found of us (Deuteronomy 4:29)! Conversely, if we do not seek God with all our mind, soul and strength of heart or imagination, He will not be found of us!

To know the God of our fathers, to develop a personal knowledge of Him, we must be acquainted with and understand His ways. We must appreciate, heed and cherish His presence. We are to serve God with a willing mind and a perfect heart full of love. God is constantly searching our heart and mind to see where our thoughts (imaginations) are located, as well as what they are focused on. If we are determined to seek and inquire of God first and foremost, we will find Him. But if we cast Him aside for some other source, He will not be found waiting for us (see 1 Chronicles 28:9). The covenant of salvation requires that we seek the Lord with diligence. We must desire Him with all our soul, focused mind, strong will and emotions in order to prosper (see 2 Chronicles 15:12).

The covenant of salvation requires that we seek the Lord with diligence.

Those who invite the Holy Spirit to come live within their being discern that the Spirit of Christ has united them into the oneness of God. Through their salvation (believing in Jesus) and placement of hope and trust in His eternal power, Believers are able to apprehend and demonstrate Jesus' love, wisdom and miracle power here on earth. The glory found in the Word of God has the final say over every one of life's situations. Most assuredly, *I say to you, he who believes in Me, the works that I do he will do also; and greater works than these he will do, because I go to My Father* (John 14:12).

The imagination is a vital key that helps us develop the artful skill of becoming successful in prayer. In that regard, prayer is much like a visionary dream state. Prayer requires the mind to be at peace, resting in a tranquil setting, in order to hear the still, small voice of Christ, see the Father's actions and receive divine wisdom from the Holy Spirit. Prayer mimics sleep by placing us in a relaxed, spiritually receptive state in order to hear the higher thoughts, see the creative directives and feel the impressions and suggestions of the Holy Spirit's presence and expressions.

The secret place of the Spirit where we pray to God is private. The Holy Spirit generously rewards us for spending focused, worshipful time in His presence. He openly manifests the results of the words we whisper for only His ears to hear.

> *When you pray, enter into your closet* (the subconscious), *and when you have shut the door* (removed sin, unforgiveness, doubt, unbelief, obstructions, distractions, confusion), *pray to the Father which is in secret; and the Father which sees* (you assuming the feeling of possessing your prayer focus) *in secret, shall reward you openly* (by causing the answer to your prayer to be realized publicly) (Matthew 6:6).

The creative sculpting of prayer is done in secret. God incentivizes the diligent, private efforts of our concealed, hidden away, imaginably inspired faith. The Holy Spirit exhibits His visible power by displaying the gifts of the Spirit moving through us. As we mature in the Spirit of the Lord, the manifestations of wisdom, understanding, counsel, might, knowledge, signs, wonders and miracles appear and flow forth on a regular basis.

The Bible is full of prayerful examples taught by Jesus. He taught His disciples to pray in a manner that would cause the kingdom of heaven's will to be done on earth. As Jesus finished praying in a certain place, one of His disciples asked Jesus to teach them to pray as John the Baptist had taught his disciples. Jesus said to His disciples:

> *When you pray, say: "Our Father in heaven may the glory of Your name be the hallowed center platform from which we live our lives. May Your Holy Spirit Kingdom come upon us, to cleanse us, so that we are empowered to manifest and do Your will on earth, as it is in heaven. Give us the spiritual bread of revelation that we need for the coming days. Forgive us of our sins, as we forgive everyone who is indebted to us, and those who have continually wronged us. And rescue us from every temptation, and deliver us from evil every time we face tribulation"* (Luke 112–4).

Then Jesus gave this illustration:

> *Imagine what would happen if you were to go to one of your friends at midnight to pound and bang on his door, ring his doorbell and shout, "Please! Do you have three loaves of bread*

to lend and some extra food you can spare? A friend of mine just arrived from a journey at my house unexpectedly and I have nothing to serve him." But your friend says, "Why are you bothering me? The door's locked and my wife (subconscious) *and kids* (imaginative ideas) *and I* (conscious) *are all in bed. Do you really expect me* (conscious) *to get up, unlock the door and give you* (prayer) *our food?" But listen—because of your shameless impudence, even though it's the middle of the night, your friend will get up out of his bed and give you* (prayer) *all that you need because of your brass persistence! So, it is with your prayers. Ask and keep on asking and you'll receive. Seek and keep on seeking and you'll discover and find what you are looking for. Knock on heaven's door, and keep knocking and one day every door will be opened for you. Every persistent person who keeps asking will get what he asks for. Every persistent seeker will discover and find what he needs. And everyone who keeps knocking persistently will one day find all the doors they knocked on are finally open to them* (Luke 11:5–10).

Another example is the encounter John the Revelator had when he saw Jesus reveal Himself in His redeemed body. John had been banished to the Isle of Patmos for preaching the Word of God. He was caught up in the Spirit on the Lord's Day. John heard the loud trumpeting voice of many waters raging with a sharp, cutting and two-edged clarity of a sword behind him. The positioning of the voice indicated that John had already entered another dimension through (the spiritual door) Jesus. John looked to see. Therein his midst, John the Revelator saw the Son of Man standing within the seven brilliant, rainbow-colored pillars of fiery light. These seven illuminating, radiating, enlightening revelatory lights infused the mind of the beholder with the divine mind of God.

> *The imagination is a vital key that helps us develop the artful skill of becoming successful in prayer.*

The prayers of John pulled him through the natural realm until he stood in a blessed place, in another spiritual dimension. There he was surrounded by the echoes of prophecy, grace and peace from the Ancient One, who is, who was and who is to come. John was joined by the seven burning eyes of divinely perfect spirits that radiated with the full spectrum of multicolored flames before the Throne of God. The noble Spirit of the Lord rose supreme.

The Spirit of Wisdom joined His spiritual perceptions, prudence and discernment in unity with the empathetic kindness of the Spirit of Understanding. The guiding Spirit of Counsel merged to encourage and give direct instruction, being fused with the powerful Spirit of Might, to carry out great exploits of valor. The Spirit of Knowledge linked its expert awareness and spiritual comprehension and was bound to the Fear of the Lord. These seven divine spirits formed a perfect circle of influence in the midst of seven burning pillars.

Imagine yourself being there with John, seeing Jesus, the Son of Man, clothed in a floor-length garment that girded His chest with a golden band. Jesus' hair glistening brilliant white, and His eyes flashing blue with the hottest flames of fire while alternating with the other six colors of rainbow light. You want to bow down and kiss His beautiful, brass-appearing feet that carried the gospel message, having been refined in the furnace of affliction on our behalf. His entire countenance is lit up like that of the sun's shining in its full strength at noonday.

Prayer mimics sleep by placing us in a relaxed, spiritually receptive state in order to hear the higher thoughts, creative directives and suggestions of the Holy Spirit's presence and expressions.

Now step back and observe John as he falls before the resurrected Son of Man. Watch as Jesus places His right hand under John's shoulder to help him to his feet. "Do not be afraid, John. IAM the First and the Last. IAM He who lives and was dead. Behold, IAM alive forevermore. I have the keys of Hades and of death. Write the things that you have seen in the multidimensional realms of the past, the things that are now in the present and the mysteries that will take place after this in a future time of existence."

Prayer requires us to utilize the power of imaginative, focused faith. We do this by joining the wisdom of God with His spiritual understanding. When we see and agree with what God is doing, we are able to ignite all of the creative forces that are found in our imagination. God is not moved by the prayers of those who use the vain repetition of formulated words found in superstitious mantras (in hopes that their incantations will have some type of magical result). Our prayerful imagination enables us to see the answers to and to feel the power of the things we are praying.

The eyes of our heart empower the seven flaming, fiery spiritual eyes of the imagination to look beyond the natural in order to see the things we hope for that are already resting in the future. Then in faith, believing that we have already received them, we usher the future into our Now!

From before the foundation of the world, the answers to our prayers have been reserved for us in another realm of the Spirit. All we have to do is activate its transference into the tangible world by using our faith and speaking the Word. That which we seek to acquire has always been in God. We are not waiting on God to deliver the answers to our prayers. God is waiting on us to discover how to enter into His many mansions to receive the vast treasures presently there waiting for us to plunder.

God speaks positive, life-giving words to us every day. God tells us, "I love you with an everlasting love. I long to spend quality time with you, My beloved! You are precious in My sight!" But so often we do not believe what God says about us. To receive the keys that will unlock our inheritance in the Kingdom of God, we must believe what God says about us is true. We must stop believing our own negative inner voice and other discouraging voices that surround us in the world of defeat. We have a choice to make. Will we believe what God says is true? Or will we believe what we think about our own self and the critical naysayers?

There is a brilliant key (we must believe God) that unlocks the treasures of today and all of our tomorrows. When we live a life of faith to its fullness each and every day, we experience the joy of the Lord moving in our life. Then we know that all of our tomorrows will bring about our expectant vision of hope a prosperous future. Facing each day with a new increased measure of faith allows us to cast our burdens on Christ and soar forward to discover the beauty that is held in each new day.

> *The creative sculpting of prayer is done in secret.*

Sometimes we have to take the golden keys of access back into the past to unlock Pandora's Box. There, we must refute and renounce all false statements and judgments that were made by us, to us, about us, through us and around us. When the mighty wind of forgiveness blows, all of the dust or confusion goes away, leaving a pure heart that is the gilded key of destiny in our clean hands.

These kingdom keys empower us to unlock our greatest destiny, so our latter days will be greater than our former. We take on the image of Christ, becoming His brothers and sisters, joint heirs and beloved Bride. We see the hope of glory. We hear the creative words God speaks over our life. Then, once and for all, we believe that what God says about us is true. Then taking all that we were, all that we have and all that we are, we lay every failure and victory at His nail-scared feet, and we pick up Christ's identity. God has placed one condition on the Believer—only believe! *Therefore, I say to you, whatever things you ask when you pray, believe that you receive them, and you will have them* (Mark 11:24).

> *As we mature in the Spirit of the Lord, the manifestations of wisdom, understanding, counsel, might, knowledge, signs, wonders and miracles appear and flow forth on a regular basis.*

By focusing our first love and desire on Jesus and forgiving others, we lessen, deafen and totally remove the effects of our negative internal voice. We need to also learn how to shut our ears to the angry, external voices that arise from others in our outer world. Connecting with God and becoming one with Him cleanses us from sin and removes all doubt, fear and unbelief. Skillfully using our God-given, creative imagination in prayer is the key that gives us access to Jesus, the only true door to Father God.

The essence of prayer is faith that believes as Jesus does. The understanding that it is the Christ within us that gives us access to the realms of glory brings us into a position to seek the wisdom of God. We are to seek wisdom, and, in all of our getting, we are to access the divine coupling of the understanding of God. Faith-filled prayer that is in total agreement with God's plans and desires is the key that gives us access to enter into the doors, to open up the windows of heaven's mansions and to call forth the pouring out of all of God's blessings upon our life. God is a rewarder of those who diligently seek Him, believe as He believes and faithfully obey

Him.

When the Spirit of the Lord is resting upon us in prayer, the seven dimensions of His Spirit are released to us as complementary couples that touch, intertwine and agree with and work alongside the other to strengthen and enhance the power of their divine partner. The Spirit of Wisdom dances with the Spirit of Understanding. The Spirit of Counsel aligns and joins hands with the strong arm of the Spirit of Might to lift up, display and carry out what they have been shown. The Spirit of Knowledge empowers the Reverential (and obedient) Fear of the Lord (see Isaiah 11:2).

The Bible teaches us to do the same with people. We learn to prefer the good and hate the evil in one another by being authentic in our brotherly and sisterly love for others. Believers should be the first to honor others by putting them first, above themselves. We should be patient and long-suffering in prayer so that people have time to repent.

There was a time when God required me to wait eight (the resurrection power of new beginnings) long, hard years for a certain personal situation to change. Even after this designated span of time had passed, the people involved still refused to communicate or change. Instead, they conspired to sabotage. It became obvious that the situation was growing from worse to dire. It was only then that God finally allowed me to forgive and release them, to separate from them and move on. Vindication came very quickly, and things immediately turned around for the better. Doors of opportunity that had been shut for years sprang wide open with invitations of favor pouring in.

Prayer requires us to utilize the power of imaginative, focused faith.

Perpetually dwelling at rest (in a state of peace) causes revelation knowledge to spring up from deep within us. After the resurrection, Jesus was seen by hundreds of people. When Jesus passed through the locked door to visit His disciples, He decreed:

> *Be at peace. Stop being cowardly, agitated, disturbed, fearful or intimidated. My own measure of peace I bequeath to you. Do not let your hearts be troubled or afraid. If a person*

> *or house is worthy or deserving, leave peace in it. We are the living houses or holy temples of God that are to abide in God's peace* (Matthew 10:11–13).

As we focus our mind and thoughts on Jesus, He floods our heart with His overwhelming peace. We are then able to lay hands on others, pray for them and impart the peace of God into their weary souls.

To gain peace, we must enter into the Spirit to rest by strengthening our level of trust in God. We enter into the presence of Jesus through peaceful prayers of thanksgiving. *By this we come to know perceive, recognize, and understand that we abide live and remain in Him and He in us; because He has given imparted to us of His Holy Spirit* (1 John 4:13).

A relaxed, prayerful state of meditation focused on the beautiful face of Jesus brings us into a peaceful state of resting in His Word. When we enter into a tranquil state of being with clean hands that have not touched evil and a pure heart of love that thinks no wrong of others, we will see Jesus.

Once we awaken our imagination to see Jesus, we will become loving like He is, and we will take on the creative power of His Spirit's image. We take on the image of Christ Jesus as we walk side by side with Him, while holding His beautiful, nail-scared hands and intimately fellowshipping with Him. When we are one with Jesus, we are fully and tenderly enveloped by Him. Now we mirror His every move from within the heart of His presence as He lovingly carries us within His glorious countenance through the garden paths of life.

> *To receive the keys that will unlock our inheritance in the Kingdom of God, we must believe what God says about us is true.*

As we continue to abide centered in Christ, we learn how to search out the mysteries He placed within the depths of the inner chambers of our subconscious. We see everything and everybody through His all-seeing eyes of love.

Let Us Pray

Holy Spirit, teach us to pray without ceasing so that we remain connected to the eternal realms of God's Spirit. Tune our spiritual ears to listen, and empower our regenerated spirits so that we feel Your presence and recognize Your three-in-one voice. Reveal Your wisdom that is found in the secret, hidden things. Teach us to focus in Your presence until we can discover and unlock the mysteries of God. Align our hearts with Yours, and give us the skills that are necessary to gain access and wisdom to operate the keys to Your glorious Kingdom. Let our eyes see the glory that is found in Your living words. Teach us to use our sanctified imaginations and imaginative, focused faith so that we are successful in the secret place of prayer. Help us to focus our first love and desire on Jesus.

We forgive others who have done us wrong, and we turn a deaf ear to all negative voices. We ask that You cleanse us by removing all doubt, unbelief and fear. Awaken our imaginations to see Jesus, fellowship with Him and believe as He does, mirroring His every move. Let us see everything and everyone through Jesus' eyes of love. Amen.

CHAPTER SEVEN

Imaginative Prayer

Imaginative prayer is the artful joining of the imagination of the conscious mind of man with the imaginative expressions of the subconscious parts of man's consciousness to God.

> *I can of Myself* (consciousness) *do nothing. As I hear, I judge; and My judgment is righteous, because I do not seek My own will but the will of the Father* (subconscious) *who sent Me* (consciousness) (John 5:30).

Imaginative prayer awakens dormant concepts. When awakened, they can resurrect into a living, viable form that we readily recognize.

> *Then Jesus answered and said to them, "Most assuredly, I say to you, the Son* (conscious) *can do nothing of Himself, but what He sees the Father* (subconscious) *do; for whatever He* (subconscious) *does, the Son* (conscious) *also does in like manner"* (John 5:19).

Imaginative prayer is the master key that unlocks every physical realm on earth. Imaginative prayer gives our imaginative subconscious entrance into the vast supplies of heaven's spiritual storehouses. These master keys of imaginative prayer open the doors that enhance our levels of imaginative faith.

> *"Bring all the tithes into the storehouse, that there may be food in My house, and try Me now in this," says the Lord of hosts. "If I will not open for you the windows of heaven and pour out for you such blessing that there will not be room enough to receive it"* (Malachi 3:10).

God's presence enables us to feel the leading of the Holy Spirit breathing ever so gently upon our subconscious. We tune our ears to listen for the whispers of His still, small voice telling us what to ask for in prayer. Whatever we see, feel and receive by the Holy Spirit, whether it is literal or symbolic, must be believed and portrayed as true in order for it to flow from the invisible fields of imaginative faith into our tangible waking lives.

Imaginative prayer brings into existence those things that have been waiting concealed and reserved for us in the invisible realms of the Spirit. When we are unified as one in Spirit and moving as we see God move, we have entered into a higher state that is activated by seeing things with the eyes of our imaginative faith. Great faith believes that All Things are possible for us when we are walking in the glory of God's surrounding love. Our prayers are answered when we assume the feelings that we are already that new person in Christ.

Through faith-filled, imaginative prayer, we take on the same image and likeness of Christ, who is in possession of our objectives. When the subconscious feels our new identity is a done deal or fact, it will create the means necessary to cause its earthly realization. Although, if we only look to see the concrete things of earth as our abiding reality, we deny the truth that through God All Things are possible.

> *Imaginative prayer is the artful joining of the imagination of the conscious mind of man with the imaginative expressions of the subconscious parts of man's consciousness to God.*

To experience a successful prayer life that manifests answers, our subconscious and conscious reality must be in total agreement with each other; there is no room for conflict or disagreement. Prayer does not attract or invite what our will wants. Prayer catches the attention of, creates an opening for and then draws to us what we believe is true! The attraction of our hopes and the actualization of our desires do not come by the strength of our willpower. The manifestation of a truth or reality is not by might; it is not by our potential or capability. Answers to prayer come to us only by the Spirit of the Lord.

Answered prayers cause us to feel loved and cared for, joyfully empowered, protected and successful. When we petition God in prayer, we should do so in the position of the sustained quality of imaginative faith. As the offsprings and Sons of God, we are heirs who live, move and reside in Christ (see Acts 17:28).

The Holy Spirit is the only helper we need to facilitate us obtaining answers to our prayers. When we are able to sustain the belief that we already possess the things we have only seen in vision form, we are able to actualize that spiritual sphere in our waking, physical world. Believing God and His living Word gives us a firm, balanced foundation for the expression of our intentional emotions and spiritual responses to the physical facts that form and influence our waking life.

Imaginative prayer gives our imaginative subconscious entrance into the vast supplies of heaven's spiritual storehouses.

Imaginative prayer successfully modifies and enlarges the frame of our mind so that we change the physical actions that animate us. When we practice imaginative prayer, we are able to deny our physical senses; for greater is He that is in us than he that is in the world. Through the power of imaginative prayer, we can believe what the Word of God says is true.

Prayer empowers the imaginative subconscious to give our spirit man the life needed to believe the rhema Word of God as fact. The conscious mind deals with the logos Word of God, the letter of the law as legal, actual evidence provided to the subconscious. We gain understanding of the Word of God as rhema reality through the feelings we experience when different ideas, principles and foundational truths and statements are received and transmitted to the imaginative subconscious.

Your personal, subconscious thoughts about other people are intuitively transferred or communicated to their subconscious. This transference takes place without their permission, agreement or conscious awareness. The subjective manner by which you view someone can affect his or her thoughts, behaviors and outlook on life. When you are praying for yourself, something or someone else, you must remove all wrong judgments, criticisms, personal conflicts, unforgiveness, bitterness or disagreements.

It is crucial to shift your focus beyond from what is displayed in the natural realm to what is being manifested in the eternal, ever-expanding dimensions of the Spirit in order to discover a higher, divine truth. Focus on what the Word of God says about your situation or what your current desire should be. Concentrate on how you will feel when your prayer is answered. Take on the image, actions and mannerisms that you would display upon receiving the realization of your prayerful desire.

Imaginative prayer is successful when it is a joint venture between our conscious faith, which believes All Things are possible with God, and our subconscious faith, which is able to manifest what it sees or feels in the imagination. The Believer obtains the things that he or she desires by keeping his or her imaginative faith focused on the end result. The creative imagination must be trained on manifesting the answer. All doubtful reasoning must be denied and renounced.

> *When we rest in a tranquil place of imaginative prayer, the eyes of our spirit are opened to see a clear vision of our inner spirit man revering God.*

We do not attract to us the things we want, but we attract the things that are already true about us. Like attracts like. We draw the things we believe are possible to obtain, while we repel that which we believe to be impossible to obtain. We subconsciously invite others who have taken on the same form, beliefs and actions we exhibit. Others are drawn to us because they are on the same path; they resonate with the same sound, and their goals resemble our own. If we can believe we will receive the results of our imaginative prayers, All Things are possible. *Jesus said to him, "If you believe, all things are possible to him who believes* (Mark 9:23).

When we believe by accepting the end result of what we have imagined as truth, Jesus (door) hears our knock, opens the door and comes streaming through to sit, dine and commune with us. He brings clarity and understanding about the answered prayer (see Revelation 3:20). Imagination sees by faith, and then it creates, forms and molds the images and likenesses required out of the fluid substance of faith. It is the Spirit that gives life and substance to all that exists. The letter of the law not only awakens our carnal knowledge but also eventually kills us. It is the Spirit that gives us a lavish life that is full.

When we rest in a tranquil place of imaginative prayer, the eyes of our spirit are opened to see a clear vision of our inner spirit man revering God. The fear of God is the beginning of wisdom. God's wisdom is not of this world. It is a launching platform that propels us into a future dimension of greatness. I know that whatever God does, it shall be forever. Nothing can be added to it, and nothing taken from it. God does it, that men should fear before Him (Ecclesiastes 3:14).

Vision connects our mind's eye (the heart or imagination) with the telling images and productive, life-giving actions of the Holy Spirit. Through imaginative visions, we are able to see God. Like Jesus, we can observe what the Father is doing so that we can respond to Him in kind and like manner. The Holy Spirit, who is continually speaking to the heart of our inner spirit man, opens our ears to hear the still, small voice of the Holy Spirit. Imaginative prayer not only causes our spirit to hear the voice of God, but it also causes us to become more receptive to seeing, sensing and recording a myriad of different spiritual impressions.

Let Us Pray

Holy Spirit, please join our imagination with our conscious and subconscious mind to awaken dormant concepts, to resurrect every part of our being into Your image and likeness. Give us the kingdom keys to see the invisible, hidden realms. Furnish us the wisdom to unlock both the physical and spiritual realms so that we can tap into earthly riches and heaven's vast supplies–so that our storehouses are full and running over. Grant us the ability to think higher, loving thoughts about ourself and others. Teach us how to keep our imagination focused on the end results so that we may prosper in all of our ways. Amen.

CHAPTER EIGHT

Supernatural Faith

When we are tested and learn to understand the ways of God and agree with the plans and purposes He has for our life, we are promoted. God rewards us with a greater measure of imaginative faith. Imaginative faith is a spiritual ability to see by the eyes of faith through our image center or imagination. A vaster measure of faith will influence, empower and enable us to use a superior amount of spiritual authority to produce more of God's will in prayer.

To receive what we ask for in prayer, we must first prepare the soil of our heart or imagination. Imaginative faith causes us to believe that (through God and the power of His Word) we have the capacity to obtain, accept and fulfill our request. Imaginative faith gives us the sense of knowing that we have heard and seen and have already received the answer to our prayer. Feeling, believing and acting like we have received the answer to our prayer will cause the evidence of the desired changes to appear.

The degree of successful results we attain are due to the measure of our confident, expectant imaginative faith that we exercise when praying. Failure to receive an answer to prayer is often because we believe what our natural, carnal senses tell us is impossible, or we employ too much intellect and not enough Spirit of Faith. Failure also comes when we do not engage our emotion of love with the person for whom we are praying, or we do not engage our emotion of love with God, for God is love.

The Power of Love

When we learn to love people unconditionally by only thinking thoughts about them that are kind, gracious, true, pure, lovely and of a good report, we will awaken those attributes in them. Our love will make it possible to give them beauty for their ashes and to exchange joy for their mourning and suffering. Supernatural faith is clothed in supernatural love.

When we gaze at our neighbors through the lens of love, we can see their lack, their desperation and their needs. When we move in compassion to resolve others' needs, we are given the wisdom to understand things from both sides of an argument. Love empowers us to see them reaching their potential in God. The person who holds a contrary view, false belief or an opposing opinion simply lacks God's internal wisdom and truth.

When we love others, we free them from a prison of limitation. Our love sets them free from damaging opinions. Love empowers people to break the harmful cords that bind them. Love empowers people to thrive in a new environment that is full of limitless possibilities. Love becomes the supportive wind beneath their wings, which causes them to spread, rise and fly to new heights.

The eyes of those who are unenlightened gaze life through the crippling scales of fear because God's love has not yet opened their calloused eyes to see truth clearly. Never allow fear to keep you from exploring something new. Life gets dull and boring when we stay safe inside the narrow boundaries of the known. By prayerfully exploring the different outcomes and imagining the possibilities that each option presents, Believers are able to gain wisdom. Love empowers us to reach an optimal level of understanding of the possible solutions that are available to form success.

Love empowers us to reach an optimal level of understanding of the possible solutions that are available to form success.

The knowledge of the ways of the Divine empowers the Believer to relate God's truth to sinners. A godly vision can come to heal lack, set the captive free and open the eyes of the blind. *"Let none of you think evil in your heart against your neighbor; and do not love a false oath. For all these are things that*

I hate," says the Lord (Zechariah 8:17). If we view others through our natural, physical eyes, we will see neither the truth of who they are currently nor who they are destined to become.

Only by looking through the spiritual eyes of love can we behold a person's God-given calling, to see their true beauty and clearly discern the truth of their full potential. Then we are able to prophetically release it. When we apply love and decree godly wisdom to reason, truth will always prevail. Opponents become allies when they agree that truth cannot be enclosed or limited by what seems to be a present fact. The scenes of our outer world are a projection that comes from our inner beliefs. They cause the mental focuses of our current imagination to appear as real.

I served as a volunteer in a maximum security prison ministry for sixteen years. These men were serving the most extreme sentences possible according to the law. In order for me to pray for and prophesy to them in faith, I had to look past their current bondage and limitations to see the untapped potential God had placed within them. I prophesied to one inmate that he would get a guitar, learn to play and write music that would be published. Although it seemed impossible that it could happen based on his current situation, it did happen! Just as God had said it would be in the prophetic word, it happened. He is now a published music and song writer while serving out his life sentence for murder. He did not deny Christ by focusing on his life sentence behind bars. Instead, his faith agreed with God, which brought his desire into a reality and a fact of blessing in his life.

Only by looking through the spiritual eyes of love can we behold a person's God-given calling, to see their true beauty and to clearly discern the truth of their full potential.

The perfect man is disciplined in all his ways. He is in tune with the timing of the still, small voice of the Holy Spirit. In the realm of God's glory, it is easy to listen to the voice of our spirit adoringly worshipping God. Communing in God's love causes us to respond to the Holy Spirit. The perfect man knows that God consciousness is the only true reality in life. It's never only about being perfect. It's about being determined to put forth your best effort every single minute of your life. A spirit of excellence brings forth changes that transform us into our highest possible level of being. To be the best, we must be able to overcome the worst with grace and dignity. Choose to take the chance to make the changes you need to be successful.

Obtaining Answers

When we first see and discern the answer to our imaginative prayer, it empowers us to rejoice. Displaying great joy and sincere thanksgiving for God's goodness releases the multiplication of blessings in our waking life. The Holy Spirit loves to spend time communicating with us. He enjoys bringing us into the eternal loop of the Trinity by narrating to us what is happening in the invisible realms of the Spirit. The Holy Spirit becomes the divine director who casts vision onto the movie screen of our heart. He transposes His creative thoughts and actions onto our subconscious imagination.

Focused, faith-filled imaginative prayer and imaginative decrees are keys that open the doors to the many mansions in the Father's house. These same imaginative prayer keys also master the entrances to all of the doors currently locked in the earthly realms. Every motion is commenced, increased and accelerated or hindered, stopped and canceled by prayer. Imaginative prayer is the key to every spiritual dimension and natural realm of existence.

Because imaginative prayer is full of God's great faith, it moves the hand of God.

Because imaginative prayer is full of God's great faith, it moves the hand of God. Nothing can stop the hand of God from moving on our behalf, for His powerful hand holds the entire universe.

> *All the inhabitants of the earth are reputed as nothing; He does according to His will in the army of heaven and among the inhabitants of the earth. No one can restrain His hand or say to Him, "What have You done"* (Daniel 4:35)*?*

Imaginative prayer turns our face toward God's, making it easy to place all of our faith in the power of His might.

When we enter into a reverent state of restful meditation, we are again promoted in God's spiritual empire. The increase we experience depends on the measure of God that we are willing and able to believe. If we stay focused on bringing the observable displays of God into our life, we will acquire an inordinate measure of imaginative faith.

To become skilled in the art of gaining answers to our prayers, we must practice extended times of restful prayer in the presence of God.

Personal Reflection Moment

Here's what I would like you to do when you pray:

1. Find a quiet, secluded, private place or go into a room and close the door so that you won't be tempted to role-play before God. Just be there as simply and honestly as you can manage. The focus will shift from you to God as you begin to sense His grace.
2. Now earnestly and honestly express your love for Him. As you are unseen by man, pray to your Father who is also unseen. Then your Father, who sees you in the secret place, will reward you openly before men (see Matthew 6:6).

We should learn how to humbly go into and gracefully bow out of His presence with our praise and thanksgiving. As our mind becomes peaceful, we enter into a time of tranquil rest.

> *Open the gates that the uncompromisingly righteous nation which keeps her faith and her trust with God may enter in. You will guard him and keep him in perfect and constant peace whose inclination and character of the mind is stayed on You, because he commits himself to You, leans on You, and hopes confidently in You. So, trust in the Lord commit yourself to Him, lean on Him, hope confidently in Him forever; for the Lord God is an everlasting Rock, the Rock of Ages* (Isaiah 26:1–4).

Have you not discerned, understood and not know that you are the temple of God, His sanctuary and that the Spirit of God has His permanent dwelling in you individually and also as a church collectively (1 Corinthians 3:16).

God created our bodies as a habitation for His presence in which to dwell. *Do you not know that your bodies are members of Christ* (1 Corinthians 6:15).

We are to work out our salvation with fear and trembling. We should be assured of our salvation if, indeed, we have truly been saved. *Examine yourselves as to whether you are in the faith. Test yourselves. Do you not know yourselves that Jesus Christ is in you?—Unless indeed you are disqualified* (2 Corinthians 13:5).

Inspired Hope

We learned about the spiritual fourth dimension in the previous volume. I will refer to and further develop concepts of the workings of the four-dimensional realm of the Spirit here and in following sections, as it pertains to being able to fully obtain and retain our new, Christlike identity or state of being. Please refer to the Realm of the Spirit and Doors to Dimensions chapters in Volume II for reference on how to access and operate in the realm of the Spirit.

God's Spirit uses the gateway of the imagination and prayer, visions and dreams to connect us to the creative energy systems of God. *Such knowledge is too wonderful for me; it is high, I cannot attain it* (Psalm 139:6).

Being adapted to the image of Christ, we discover the spiritual doors of access that have always been there waiting for us to ask, seek and knock upon until we are granted entrance. These dimensional doors are only seen by and accessible to us when we are at oneness with that particular aspect, characteristic or dimension of Christ Jesus. He cannot share His glory with another. We must be one with Him, just as Jesus is one with His Father. We become truly one with Christ when we clothe ourselves in His divine love, taking on the same images of His likeness, character and attributes.

> *Placing our expectant hope in Christ empowers us to assume the mental position we have already seen, experienced and possessed.*

This is what the Bible denotes when it states that whatever we (the Bride) desire (the Groom, Jesus) to be, when we pray and believe that we have already received it, we shall be given it, take on that image and be it (see

Mark 11:24). Prayer is the art of realizing you are that which you desire to be. It is not begging and pleading with God for your desires.

Prayer is placing our hope in Christ. Prayer is believing that through Him All Things are possible. When we are conscious of being one with the Creator, it is the most intimate, ecstatic experience. It is like a spiritual wedding where we are romanced by the Divine. As the Bride, the eternal spirit of mortal man, we relinquish our current name, characteristics and identity to receive a *new name*. In God's loving embrace, we are impregnated with His characteristics, divine nature and identity.

Hope is the lifeline that requires the use of one's imagination to visualize the substance of what is desired.

Placing our expectant hope in Christ empowers us to assume the mental position we have already seen, experienced and possessed. Hope is the lifeline that requires the use of one's imagination to visualize the substance of what is desired. The power of our hope draws that which rests in the jurisdiction of the Spirit into the natural realm. *Now faith is the substance of things hoped for, the evidence of things not seen* (Hebrews 11:1).

The world and all of creation is contained within our internal visual scope of our imagination. In order for the answers to our prayers to manifest, we must first believe to see, hear, feel and be aware of their existence. Then we must imagine, exercise our faith and expect what is actually possible. That which we desire to experience is activated by God's resurrection power when our imaginative faith gives it life. *Hope deferred makes the heart sick, but when the desire comes, it is a Tree of Life* (Proverbs 13:12).

Miracles work according to the measure of faith one possesses. Imaginative faith is the creative force that makes it possible to attain what we desire.

> *I sent you to harvest a field where you did not sow. Without lifting a finger, you have walked in on a field worked long and hard by others who have labored, and you have entered into their labors* (John 4:38).

Faith, wisdom and understanding are the triple cords of power that must be united within our being in order to become the threefold key that unlocks various doors. These doors give us entrance into the mansions of the different ascending dimensions of glory. We enter into the mansion of imaginative faith to receive wisdom. We enter into the mansion of wisdom to gain understanding of how to move into the territories of glory. What we glean or receive in one or another mansion is then added to us. The revelation knowledge we receive will help us advance to higher mansions or states of being when we activate our imaginative faith in order to use what we have learned.

Behind each of these seven-dimensional mansion doors rest untold, creative treasures of faith, spiritual counsel, divine knowledge, understanding, wisdom and glorious might found in the reverent fear of God. *And there shall be stability in your times, an abundance of salvation, wisdom, and knowledge; the reverent fear and worship of the Lord is your treasure and His* (Isaiah 33:6). When we peacefully rest in these spiritual dimensions with faith-filled expectation, we will resurrect hope and inherit that estate in our waking life. By using our imaginative faith, we can create, breathe in the breath of life and maintain any state of being we can believe, hope for or imagine.

We pray in imaginative faith to gain the divine wisdom of God, which is not of this world. God's pure wisdom is more valuable than the finest of gold that has been tried in the fires of affliction. Imaginably motivated prayer gives us spiritual understanding, which is far better than the highest quality of sterling silver. Faith, wisdom and understanding are the principal entities that empower us to astonish man with God's grandeur by performing the mighty, miraculous works of God in and through His Spirit (see Proverbs 4:5, 7; 16:16; 19:8; Matthew 13:54; Mark 6:2).

> *The presence of the Holy Spirit resting upon our subconscious opens up all of our spiritual gateways and senses.*

We maintain our adoration of God by focusing our imagination on His beauty, stateliness, magnificence and excellent greatness. The words we choose to magnify the Lord should be stately, fit for a Monarch, creative and varied. Never use the same old religious routine or vain repetition. God deserves our very best creative expressions. We are to love and honor His Majesty.

In this prayerful and imaginative state, we prepare our spirit to receive the audible, visual and physical impressions of the breath of the Spirit. Therefore, whatsoever you have spoken in darkness shall be heard in light; and that which you have spoken in the ear in closets shall be proclaimed upon the housetops (Luke 12:3).

When the Holy Spirit removes another veil, all of our senses are enlightened, activated and empowered to receive fresh, bright impressions from God. We see clear visions, perceive dreams and accept the touch of spiritual signs that transform us into God's image and powerful likeness. The presence of the Holy Spirit resting upon our subconscious opens up all of our spiritual gateways and senses. The subconscious empowers our spiritual ears to hear the whispers of the Holy Spirit's still, small voice. It opens the windows of our eyes to see so that our spirit can sense, reach out and touch, gather and grasp the divine wisdom of the Holy Spirit.

Let Us Pray

Father, teach us to understand Your ways. We agree with Your divine plans and purposes for our lives. Open our eyes of faith to see Your presence and the limitless realms of glory. Keep us in the center of Your perfect will. Show us how to love people unconditionally, to be kind, gracious and pure of heart. Take all of our ashes, pain and sorrow from us, and exchange them for Your beauty, compassion and wisdom. Let Your exceedingly great love break every cord that limits or binds us to the natural realms of existence. Please remove the scales of fear from our eyes so that we can see with the eyes of Your great faith. Let us see others through Your spiritual eyes in order to correctly discern the truth of their fullest potential. Help us be disciplined in all of our ways so that we will arise as the perfect person. Center us in the eternal loop of the Trinity so that we can glean from Your wisdom. Amen.

CHAPTER NINE

Imaginative Visions and Dreams

Through faith, we imagine, listen, hear, look and search out mysteries to believe and see how to discover God's secrets. Using our imagination during prayer is the master key that unlocks the unknown realms of revelation knowledge that has been waiting for us in the Spirit. This master key of imaginative prayer also opens our spirit. We can access the mysteries that have been hidden within us and bring them into our natural world.

Once we have access, we can develop a masterful prayer strategy that acts as a faith carrier or transport agent. We free and move the invisible thing that the imagination desired into the visible, tangible realm by believing it is possible, prophesying God's plans and boldly decreeing the Word. By the way of Spirit-led prophetic declaration, we make manifest the hidden anomalies of God's divine wisdom.

> *But God has revealed them to us through His Spirit. For the Spirit searches All Things, yes, and the deep things of God. For what man knows the things of a man except the spirit of the man which is in him? Even so, no one knows the things of God except the Spirit of God* (1 Corinthians 2:6–11).

My famous, informative book *When Will My Dreams Come True?* deals with the Issachar anointing for understanding the times and seasons of when mysteries will manifest. It explores the introductory, elementary echelons and escalates to the advanced stratums of revelation. This revelatory book lays out a simple, yet profound, detailed plan of how to easily capture spiritual insights, knowledge and discernment that come to us as answered prayers in our dreams and through visions. Understanding our dreams become simple and plain when we learn to write out our vision based on the revelation found in Habakkuk 2:1–3.

Visions reveal the divine nature, righteous character, loving personality and attributes of God's judgments. Christ makes Himself real to us through these vibrant, colorful and lifelike visionary encounters. True, weighty visions, though infrequent, come to break us out of limitations. When we are at the crossroads of life, visions come to set a new course that changes, remakes and elevates us. Visions cause us to gain a clear perspective of our potential.

Using our imagination during prayer is the master key that unlocks the unknown realms of revelation knowledge that has been waiting for us in the Spirit.

Visions offer keys that fulfill, enlarge, change or redirect our destiny. We hear God's voice in a vision. We can feel God's touch and commune there with Him in a face-to-face encounter. God reveals who He is to us in a vision. God sends visions to us that reveal who we are currently. More importantly, visions also divulge the person we are called to become in Christ by showing things that will take place in the distant future.

Stand and set yourself firmly on the rampart during your prayer watch of the night to look, imagine and see what God shows you. Then listen to hear what the voice of God communicates. Receive His loving correction, guidance and wisdom. Envision a new picture in your mind's eye, and activate your emotions so that they can respond as the Holy Spirit directs.

Actively wait upon the Lord in prayer. Meditate on His Word until He brings clarity to the revelation. The Holy Spirit will add to and strengthen your faith. God always operates in your best interest; therefore, keep expecting the vision to happen. Be sure to thank God for His wisdom. Then carefully write down the clear, plain steps the Holy Spirit reveals on how to achieve the vision or obtain your desire. Develop a plan that pursues a strategy and sets obvious goals to bring the manifestation of the vision into reality.

Read, contemplate and reflect on the vision. Constantly pray, decree and declare that God will bring the revelation to pass. Prayerfully keep the revelatory vision before you morning, noon and night. Peace will help you to discern the proper timing of the vision's fulfillment. It is important to write down everything that you saw happening. Then take the necessary steps of action to accomplish the vision. Do not become discouraged or weary if the vision is delayed. Keep the lamp of faith's light burning brightly.

Be expectant and remain hopeful. Do not allow any fear, unbelief or doubt to enter your heart. Doubt and unbelief are evil twins that act like kryptonite. Agreeing with any of these dark forces will destroy the vision. Never fear the consequences of doing what is just and right, for God's throne is built upon that strong foundation. You can rest in knowing that your structure is sure. His advice is sound.

Maintain a holy life of purity. Those who have a pure heart and clean hands will see God's power and presence strongly manifested on their behalf. The eyes of the Lord are searching for those who have placed their wholehearted trust in Him so that He can show Himself strong on their behalf. Sin separates us from God by erecting a barrier that steals our bold confidence to approach Him in prayer. Sin will delay the fulfillment of the vision, and if repentance doesn't come, it will postpone, cancel and ultimately destroy the vision. Repent of any sin, self-hatred, curses and iniquity. Release all unforgiveness, bitterness or negative judgments. Sin fills the soul with darkness that distorts, warps and twists us with fears that blind our eyes, and it completely blocks the manifestation of our vision.

> *By the way of Spirit-led prophetic declaration, we make manifest the hidden anomalies of God's divine wisdom.*

Continue to wait patiently upon the Lord. God will fulfill the vision in His perfect time, so be expectant and persistent, prayerfully following God's Word. Then prepare yourself to be successful by cooperating with God's amazing visions.

The Powerful Realm of Sleep

We can be awake while having a vision, or we can also be asleep (dreaming) when we have a vision. Often, we are awakened out of sleep during our visionary encounters. Dreams that we have during our sleep are a chief master key to the gateways into the Spirit realm. They give us access to our subconscious. During our dreams, the Holy Spirit discloses previews of truth. He reveals the exceeding greatness of the amazing phenomena He has planned for us in our dreams of the night (as well as through our visionary impressions). These farsighted glimpses come through the quiet witness of our spirit. Whatever we are consciously aware of becomes the reality of our world.

We spend approximately one-third of our life sleeping. In the restorative posture of sleep, our organs are still continuously at work, and our brain remains active imagining, thinking, designing, sorting and solving problems. Our heart continues to beat, circulating blood throughout the body, and our lungs actively breathe in fresh air and exhale the old. Our liver, kidneys, stomach and intestines continue to process food, extracting the vitamins and minerals for use while filtering out poisonous toxins.

Visions reveal the divine nature, righteous character, loving personality and attributes of God's judgments.

During sleep, we receive a fresh vision of an expected end. By prayerfully exercising patience, long-suffering and self-control, these fruits of the Spirit become keys that cause us to adjust our thoughts and feelings into a higher imaginative state or realm of well-being. As these keys unlock the access door to Jesus, He gives us entrance into His Father's many mansions. *May the Lord direct your hearts into* (realizing and showing) *the love of God and into the steadfastness and patience of Christ and in waiting for His return* (2 Thessalonians 3:5).

In a dream state, we can look around these grand, stately mansions. We are transformed into a new identity by taking on these unfamiliar kingdom dimensions. When we believe, we can see how to glean the revelation knowledge being presented. Seeing and moving from this kingdom dimension, we are able to prayerfully enter into, focus upon and maintain that particular mansion in the waking two-thirds of our life.

These God-given visions instill hope and fresh strategy that renews our anticipation for a prosperous life and future. Visions are also master keys that reveal God's nature, character and grand attributes so that we can know His ways and emulate His greatness. Dreams are master keys that release the heavenly designs of greatness that are held captive in our imagination. They are the architectural blueprints that show us the divine strategies and plans that God has created for us. Dreams display, investigate and explain the future concealed in our DNA. The DNA dreams that God has planted within our spirit inspire us to transcend all physical barriers, mental frontiers and emotional limitations.

Visionary dreams and prophecy always follow their interpretation. Therefore, the faith-filled words that we choose to describe what the imaginative dream means and what the prophecy indicates for our future are crucially important. Dreams will track with and adhere to their interpretation.

God promises to give His beloved sweet sleep. *He will not allow your foot to be moved; He who keeps you will not slumber. Behold, He who keeps Israel shall neither slumber nor sleep* (Psalm 121:3–4). Sleep is nature's doorway to the subconscious.

During sleep, the (female) subconscious mind joins with the (male) counterpart of the conscious mind so that she is overshadowed and impregnated with the power to conceive greatness. After the incubation time has passed, and the ideas are securely maintained in the nurturing womb, the creative ideas will continue to grow throughout the entire gestation period. The subconscious is able to conceive ideas, grow, birth and produce our beliefs as her own children. These beautiful ideas are incubated as revelation knowledge that become the children of our future.

> *The eyes of the Lord are searching for those who have placed their wholehearted trust in Him so that He can show Himself strong on their behalf.*

Children represent the fruits of our thoughts, images, promises and ideal states of being that mirror our conscious beliefs. This is how the promises of God, found in His Word, become flesh. Jesus was the living Word of God. He became flesh and blood, moved into the neighborhood and walked among us. *We actually saw His glory, honor and His majesty, such glory as the only begotten Son receives from his Father, full of grace, favor, loving-kindness and truth* (John 1:14).

The Father, Son and Holy Spirit come to take up their residence within us. Their life-giving blood courses through our bodies and empowers us to do great exploits, which demonstrate that God's glory dwells within the Sons of God.

Our subconscious is most at home when we are in an unconscious state of sleep. God visits our sleep to open the eyes of our spiritual understanding, to enhance the ability of our ears to hear His voice and to seal our instructions. *In a dream, in a vision of the night, when deep sleep falls upon men, while slumbering on their beds, then He opens the ears of men, and seals their instruction* (Job 33:15–16). The Holy Spirit inhabits us to communicate His love and to impart His plans and purposes to us during the times we fall asleep. God uses the one-third of our life sleeping to show us what will transpire in the waking two-thirds.

> Dreams that we have during our sleep are a chief master key to the gateways into the Spirit realm.

The Holy Spirit is the constant lover of our soul. He resides within us to redeem every minute. Once we receive Jesus as our Lord and Savior, the Holy Spirit will never leave or forsake us. God sticks closer than a brother because He dwells deep within us.

Personal Reflection Moment

Consider the following preparations and practices:

1. Before going to sleep, it is important to remove all negative emotions. Do not entertain thoughts of fear, worry, anxiety, depression, weariness, loneliness, sadness, judgment, resentment, rejection or anger.

2. Remember, the feminine subconscious is very impressionable. She will receive and believe the images or expressions the masculine conscious displays to her. The subconscious will not doubt, amend or try to reason with what she is shown or told. She will wholeheartedly embrace it, and she will begin the process of birthing it into existence. Therefore, the thoughts that one focuses on before entering into sleep are the ideas that will be conceived, incubated, developed

and birthed into a reality. This is why Scripture warns us not to let the sun go down on our wrath. In other words, before slipping into sleep, resolve your anger. Again, do not focus on failure, sorrow, doubt, unbelief or any other fear that produces grief or any other form of negative, conflicting energy that is a draining force.

3. Prior to falling asleep, begin using your time to produce positive outcomes instead of spinning your wheels. Prayerfully forgive yourself and any other person who has hurt you. Remove all of these destructive ideas or harmful feelings from your presence. Prayer that takes place in a restful state makes it easier to let go of the striving that tries to manipulate the outcome. When we trust in God, He is able to open the right doors at the right time to connect us to the right people in the right places.

4. Prayerfully invite and embrace the presence of God's peace, rest in His comforting embrace. Receive the blessings of His grace and love. Accept God's kindness and gentleness toward you. Allow His joy to strengthen you by the power of His might. In order to prosper, you must make positive, faith-filled confessions that boldly decree the Word of God. Look to see the things that are not yet a reality in your life. Receive them with faith as though they are now yours. Believe that you have already received them. See by faith, and put on the new robes of righteousness.

5. Assume the feelings of their reality in your waking life. Wake knowing that you have taken on the image of Christ that was displayed to you. Become that new creature in Christ. Bring the presence of heaven into being in your earthen body. Use the power of God to change your waking concepts and spiritual perceptions in order to change the world that surrounds.

We must first change by taking possession of a higher state of being. We are required to move into a larger mansion in order to access all the glorious gifts, wisdom and power that have been hidden there for us to discover. It is necessary that we are transformed into the image of Christ and that we maintain His glorious likeness. Then the world around us can see His goodness and, ultimately, be converted.

We cannot look within ourselves to access something that we do not currently know, believe or possess. We must look to Jesus, the author and finisher of our faith; for within Christ Jesus, All Things live, move and have their being. Therefore, Christ alone is the answer. We can attract everything we need from the vast depths of the Spirit of God who dwells within us. The world is continually searching for answers. People are waiting for a deliverer, a healer, a savior to arise out of the chaos of this fallen world. For a dying world to see Jesus, we must take on the image of Christ. It is our responsibility to do this in order to save a desperate humanity from destroying themselves.

It is important to journal your dreams. My ministry offers expert dream analysis to assist you in interpreting and understanding your dreams. If you would like to access this opportunity, please take a few minutes to open a password-protected online dream journal at DreamsDecoder.com or DecodeMyDream.com. You can record and submit your dreams and visions for my professional analysis.

It is important to note the waking time and date of your dream or vision. The *Waking Words of Ancient Wisdom* Dream Card (available on my personal website: BarbieBreathitt.com) will also assist you in discovering the living Word of God that will establish your prayer decrees, prophetic declarations, dreams and visions. Additionally, you may research the chapter and verse combinations found in Scripture that match the times you awoke from your dream. Write out and record the verses that relate to your waking time. The Scripture reference will help to give a spiritual foundation, insights and wisdom into the meaning of the vision. Then write out the detailed scenes of the dream and the symbols along with their meanings.

Dreams are master keys that release the heavenly designs of greatness that are held captive in our imagination.

Next submit your dreams and visions to receive a professional analysis so that you can know what God is communicating to you about your brilliant future. From the strategies that you receive from your dream analysis, you can make a plan to prayerfully walk the dream or vision out in your waking in order to prosper beyond measure.

Habakkuk 2:1–4 contains numerous insightful keys to help us awaken a personal or corporate prayer movement. The proper, accurate interpretation of visions will develop a godly justice structure that is founded on righteousness and truth. When the Church is based on God's kingdoms of faith, righteousness and justice, she will not be a weak, irrelevant, perishing institution. The vibrant, supernatural Believers made up of living stones will rise up with healing power in their wings. They will demonstrate all manner of restoration through their God-given authority to command creative miracles.

Dreams display, investigate and explain the future concealed in our DNA.

> *I will stand my watch and set myself on the rampart* (wall), *and watch to see* (imagine, dream, have visions and trances) *what He will say to me* (words of wisdom, revelation and prophecy), *and what I will answer* (repent) *when I am corrected. Then the Lord answered me and said: "Write the vision and make it plain on tablets, that he may run who reads it. For the vision is yet for an appointed time but at the end it will speak and it will not lie. Though it tarries, wait for it; because it will surely come, it will not tarry. Behold the proud, his soul is not upright in him; but the just shall live by his faith"* (Habakkuk 2:1–4).

God speaks through a vocal gift called prophecy to express His mind, will and thoughts to man. Almighty God also communicates to us what needs to take place through His brilliant visual displays. Visions demonstrate the actions that are necessary for us to fulfill the symbolic picture images that show new business deals, strategic connections and contacts for advancement, state of the art inventions, profitable investments or miracles, signs and wonders taking place.

God utilizes the realms of visions and dreams to show humanity their past mistakes for the purpose of them not being repeated. God gives dreams and visions to show us our present condition of lack so that we will ask and seek Him for provision. Dreams and visions can also reveal areas of pride, and they can show us the roots of sickness or disease. Visions can show us the snares that the enemy has laid to trip us up or cause us to fall. Visions can also show us the way of escape to keep us from falling, or they can prevent us from walking on the path that would lead to our destruction. *To bring back his soul from the pit, that he may be enlightened with the light of life* (Job 33:30).

God grants us dreams and visons so that we may know who we are destined to become. The revelatory realms come so we will praise God and give Him glory for His excellent greatness. *Awake, you who sleep, arise from the dead, and Christ will give you light* (Ephesians 5:14).

Let Us Pray

Lord, we pray that You would open up our spirits so that we can discern the great mysteries that have been concealed within us. Give us visions that reveal Your divine nature, character and holy attributes. Help us find our places on the walls of prayer so that we can decree, declare and prophesy Your Word night and day. Teach us how to be accurate stewards of Your revelation knowledge. Let us write the vision down to make it plain for others to run with great skill and understanding. We desire to live pure, holy lives with clean hands that continually serve You. Help us to be quick to repent so that we can remain in Your perfect timing. Give us sweet sleep so that we can explore the visions and interpret the dreams You sow into our spirits. Amen.

CHAPTER TEN

Believe to See!

Jesus said, "If you had known Me, you would have known My Father also; and from now on you know Him and have seen Him."

Philip said, "Lord, show us the Father and that will be enough for us."

Jesus answered: "He who has seen Me has seen the Father; so how can you say, 'Show us the Father?' Do you not believe that IAM in the Father, and the Father in Me? The words that I speak to you, I do not speak on My own authority; but the Father who dwells in Me does the works. Believe Me, that IAM in the Father and the Father in Me, or else believe Me for the sake of the works themselves. If you love Me, keep My commandments. And I will pray the Father, and He will give you another Helper, that He may abide with you forever—the Spirit of truth, whom the world cannot receive, because it neither sees Him nor knows Him; but you know Him, for He dwells with you and will be in you. I will not leave you orphans; I will come to you. A little while longer and the world will see Me no more, but you will see Me. Because I live, you will live also. At that day you will know that I am in My Father, and you in Me, and I in you. He who has My com-

mandments and keeps them, it is he who loves Me. And he who loves Me will be loved by My Father, and I will love him and manifest Myself to him."

Then Judas said, "Lord, how is it that You will manifest Yourself to us, and not to the world?"

Jesus answered and said to him, "If anyone loves Me, he will keep My Word; and My Father will love him, and We will come to him and make Our home with him. He who does not love Me does not keep My words; and the word which you hear is not Mine but the Fathers who sent Me" (John 14:7–24).

Jesus and His Father are one. They are united by the Holy Spirit as the three-in-one Trinity. Anyone who loves Jesus and keeps His Word is loved by the Father. Both Jesus and the Father come to set up their earthly home in that person's body. What an honor to being a living vessel that houses all of the Godhead. God's indwelling power is closer than the words we speak and the air we breathe. With God inhabiting our soul, nothing is impossible for us to achieve if we only believe.

The soul attracts its highest aspirations. The passionate soul draws to itself the things that it desires and focuses upon, loves, dreads and fears. However, we do not manifest that which we want to be. We manifest that which we truly believe ourself to be.

We can pray to forgive sins. We prophesy the life-giving Word of God, which has the power to transform the lives of those who receive, believe and act on the prophetic word. God has given us the spiritual intelligence and powerful kingdom keys to regenerate or transform us into whatever we desire. But if people do not believe what God's Word asserts about them is true, the life-bearing seeds of the prophetic word remain dormant. Faith is the catalytic substance that fertilizes the seeds of prayer.

> *God has given us the spiritual intelligence and powerful kingdom keys to regenerate or transform us into whatever we desire.*

Our ideas produce empathy and compassionate feelings of faith. *Then He touched their eyes and said, "According to your* (feelings) *faith, be it unto you"* (Matthew 9:29)! Our inner beliefs determine our ability to believe, see, access and obtain a new reality. If we are willing to trust God with all that we have, we will receive more than we have ever dreamed possible. In contrast, if we are stingy, even what we have will be lost or taken from us. To all who are faithful to God, even more will be given. However, the ones who have nothing, even the little they think they have will be taken from them (see Luke 19:26).

This biblical truth is evidenced in the natural by the rich becoming richer, while the poor remain destitute. Jesus said, "You will always have the poor among you!" Poverty is a scarcity, deprivation mindset that causes distress and attracts impoverished hardships. If all the wealth was forcibly stripped from the people, especially those who knew how to create and gather wealth, and a corrupt, socialist government demanded that all the wealth be distributed equally among every single person on the planet, it would not take very long until the majority of the world's money found its way back into the hands of those who know how to handle, invest, create and gather wealth.

> *Prophecy cannot manifest until it is seen in our imagination, planned and affirmed in writing, recorded on the tablets of our heart, announced through faith-filled prayer, decreed into being and then acted upon in our waking life.*

Wealth gained by dishonesty will be diminished, but he who gathers by labor will increase (Proverbs 13:11).

As for every man to whom God has given riches and wealth, and given him power to eat of it, to receive his heritage and rejoice in his labor—this is the gift of God (Ecclesiastes 5:19).

> *You might say in your heart* (imagination), *"The power and strength of my hands have made this wealth for me." But remember that it is the Lord your God who gives you the power to gain wealth, in order to confirm His covenant that He swore to your fathers, as it is this day* (Deuteronomy 8:17–18).

The testimony of Jesus is the Spirit of Prophecy. Prophecy cannot manifest until it is believed, seen and planned in our imagination, affirmed in writing, recorded on the tablets of our heart, announced through faith-filled prayer, decreed into being and then acted upon in our waking life. *We must become doers of the Word, not hearers only, deceiving ourselves* (James 1:22). Hearing the written or prophetic Word is not enough. We must believe the Word of God and activate it with our faith. Then we must develop a plan or strategy that empowers us to take action to do and become what we heard.

When sins are forgiven, their ugly, crippling influences are also removed. Repentance purifies the heart of our imagination. It changes and renews our mind. It creates a clean slate and makes room for a second chance. The reading, understanding, praying and declaration of the Word of God renew our mind. The Word of God corrects our wrong thought patterns by removing any agreement with the lies that are found in mental strongholds. The Word of God empowers us to break bad habits.

> *Therefore repent and return, so that your sins may be wiped away, in order that times of refreshing may come from the presence of the Lord. And that He may send Jesus, the Christ appointed for you, whom heaven must receive until the period of restoration of All Things about which God spoke by the mouth of His holy prophets from ancient time. Moses said, "The Lord God will raise up for you a prophet like me from your brethren; to Him you shall give heed to everything He says to you"* (Acts 3:19–22).

The old man of sin must first be crucified, laying aside his dirty garments. Then the image of the new man is conceived (born from above), incubated and formed deep within us. As we maintain our focus on our new identity, the Christ within us shows us how to keep the door open. We are created in God's image; therefore, we are to be like Him. In order to be like God, we must possess the mind of Christ.

> *Let this mind be in you which was also in Christ Jesus who being in the form of God, thought it not robbery to be equal with God, but made Himself of no reputation, taking the form of a bondservant, and coming in the likeness of men* (Philippians 2:5–8).

By imaginative faith, we reach deep within our being and take the hand of our newly-formed image to escort that innovative person into our life. We embrace this new identity with a kiss, just as we have imagined ourself being or becoming. By bringing this new identity into the land of our reality, this different person will be our fresh identity as it comes to rest transposed upon us. Because Jesus believed Himself to be equal to God, He did the works of God. Jesus said, "My Father and I are one!"

The new man that is born in Christ Jesus now dwells within us. When the old, sinful man repents and dies, our senses behold the new, sin-free self. We finally see ourself the way God has always seen us. Those with clean hands and a pure heart will ascend into a higher consciousness, where their spirit is able to believe, see, touch and know God.

We must believe the Word of God and activate it with our faith.

When we see God, we are transformed and assimilated into Christ. We are finally able to see our real self and look at others through God's eyes of love.

> *Who may ascend into the hill of the Lord? Or who may stand in His holy place? He who has clean hands and a pure heart, who has not lifted up his soul to an idol, nor sworn deceitfully. He shall receive blessing from the Lord, and righteousness from the God of his salvation* (Psalm 24:3–5).

His divine image is imprinted upon the tablets of the heart to be read by all men. *By faith he forsook Egypt, not fearing the wrath of the king; for he endured as seeing Him who is invisible* (Hebrews 11:27).

We were formed by the light of God's spoken Word. God skillfully placed a portion of eternity within each person's body as His loving hands carefully shaped us from dust. We are spiritual beings created to speak God's creative Word out of a portion of God's indwelling Ruach Spirit. We must recognize the magnificent God within us in order to know that His powerful presence within us is true.

If we are constantly looking to other people to connect us to God or do the acts of God on our behalf, we will never awaken to our own oneness in God; thus the Believer is limited by the degrees of his or her beliefs. My intellect is limited by the things I do not know or have any knowledge of in my present state of existence.

The new creature that is now dwelling in Christ Jesus awakens and emerges from within our being. He or she stands up, and the power of Christ exudes out of him or her. We have been transformed into an immortal being that will live for eternity. God exists in us so that we can live and move and have our being in Him. Because Christ is dwelling within our imagination, we can achieve anything we desire to do or be.

> *The more we learn about God, the more we are able to take on His divine nature and emulate His presence here on earth as His heavenly ambassadors.*

> *It is the power of God who has saved us and called us with a holy calling, not according to our works, but according to His own purpose and grace which was given to us in Christ Jesus before time began, but has now been revealed by the appearing of our Savior Jesus Christ, who has abolished death and brought life and immortality to light through the gospel* (2 Timothy 1:9–10).

God's Kingdom comes to us so that His will is done in us (within and through earthen vessels) on earth.

> *But you have not so learned Christ, if indeed you have heard Him and have been taught by Him, as the truth is in Jesus: that you put off, concerning your former conduct, the old man which grows corrupt according to the deceitful lusts, and be renewed in the spirit of your mind, and that you put on the new man which was created according to God, in true righteousness and holiness. Therefore, putting away lying, let each one of you speak truth with his neighbor, for we are members of one another* (Ephesians 4:20–25).

As ambassadors of the kingdom of heaven, we embody the Word of God so that we can boldly display the stateliness of His excellent greatness to others. We mirror the immensity of God's grandeur here on earth. However, the spiritual is not first. The natural man develops first and then the higher spiritual person comes.

The first man is from the earth, earthy; the second man is from heaven. As is the earthy, so also are those who are earthy; and as is the heavenly, so also are those who are heavenly. Just as we have borne the image of the earthy, we will also bear the image of the heavenly (1 Corinthians 15:46–49).

The more we learn about God, the more we are able to take on His divine nature and emulate His presence here on earth as His heavenly ambassadors.

Let Us Pray

Jesus, we pray that You will empower us to prophesy Your life-giving Word that releases the power of God to transform the lives of those who believe and act on it. As we repent, laying aside our filthy garments, and forgive others, we ask that You would remove the ugly, crippling influences of sin that have stained our lives. We ask that You would imprint Your divine nature and image upon our hearts. Teach us how to be new creatures dwelling in Christ. Thank you for saving us by Your grace and for calling us with a holy calling. We ask that Your Kingdom come and that Your will be done within each of us. Amen.

CHAPTER ELEVEN

Clear Vision

Dreams and visions reveal your heavenly identity so that it can be believed, seen, embraced and manifested here on the earth. Dreams that are correctly interpreted enable you to develop a plan to fulfill your destiny and God-given purposes in life. Jesus uses beautiful visionary images to introduce us to our true self. When we see who we are destined to be in Christ, we can be transformed to *fit in* with what God is doing. We are no longer conformed to this world. Rather, we fit together, joined bone to bone, jointed with divine connections to move forward and overflow with the creative Ruach breath of God's Spirit.

We are called to fit into God, not into society. We are not of this world, but we have been chosen to remold the world around us to fit God's kingdom mandates. Be clever and very shrewd when dealing with the world. Inquire of God on every decision. Use godly wisdom, and you will prosper. *As for me, I would seek God and inquire of and require Him, and to God would I commit my cause—Who does great things and unsearchable, marvelous things without number* (Job 5:8–9). We are created in God's image to reflect His glory.

The Holy Spirit introduces us to our truest self-identity by announcing our highest possible character and destiny. If we partner with Jesus in obedient faith and work diligently, we will be celebrated and will obtain many prizes. When we hear the prophetic proclamation of an amazing, positive and godly image coming forth, we often respond by countering God's Word with our own negative, limited and self-debasing outlook on life. Negativity is a curse that nullifies creativity. Nothing good can come from a negative attitude.

The Word of God, dreams, visions and prophecy come to cause a confrontation with our current levels of spiritual belief. Revelation increases our godly knowledge, and answered prayer enhances our character and integrity development. We can change our ways by renewing our mind by the Holy Spirit in order to evolve into a higher state being or mansion in which we dwell.

Prophecy humbles us by removing the things of pride in our life, which prevent us from trusting God and arising to manifest our future destiny. Our actions are rooted in either a positive, creative, life-giving Word of God or a negative thought pattern. Negative thoughts must be captured, cast down, repented of, permanently removed and then replaced by the life-giving, creative light of God's active Word. Positive thoughts form a constructive, responsive way of living. Negative thoughts build a harmful mental stronghold that causes sickness, disease, fear and paralysis.

Dreams that are correctly interpreted enable you to develop a plan to fulfill your destiny and God-given purposes in life.

The Bible instructs us to take every negative thought captive, to cast down vain imaginations that try to exalt themselves against the true knowledge of God. We are to use vanity as a stepping stone to propel us into a greater jurisdiction of influence. We advance through the wisdom, spiritual authority and insights we have gained from overcoming life's negative experiences.

To continue to move forward, we have to cast down our low self-esteem, victim mentality, lack of trusting others and the spirit of rejection. We must also tear down all of our cynically motivated, destructive strongholds. We must discard all of our negative, fear-based beliefs, anxiety, discouragement, depression, disappointments, doubt and worry. Job warned, *The thing that I greatly feared has come upon me* (Job 3:25).

You must stop believing the worst about yourself. Never let others dominate your life. You need to be the star decision maker who takes the driver's seat and the leading role in your own life's drama. For with God, nothing will be impossible (Luke 1:37).

We must stop identifying with the enemy's lies that keep us as a lowly, spineless, earthbound caterpillar. We, instead, must learn to believe God's truth about us. Then we will emerge as the beautiful butterfly and soar from one level of grace to another even higher level of grace. *And do not be conformed to this world, but be transformed by the renewing of your mind, that you may prove what is that good and acceptable and perfect will of God* (Romans 12:2).

The Spirit of Christ dwells in my imagination, and nothing is too difficult for Him. Therefore, if I agree with and prayerfully rest in the imaginative images God has shown to me of who I am called to be, they will manifest in me as I continue to believe in faith.

The increased standard or measure of faith that we possess will change and transform the world in which we live. Heaven is drawn to us according to the amount of Christ contained within our spirit and soul that we have discovered. Before God laid the foundation of the world, we were already present in the loins of Christ. When God created man in His own image, He preplanned the exact timing of when each would be born—their length of life, their gifting and each person's destiny (see Genesis 1:27).

> *We are not of this world, but we have been chosen to remold the world around us to fit God's kingdom mandates.*

Just as we have borne the image of the earthy, we will also bear the image of the heavenly (1 Corinthians 15:49). God the Father foreknew, predestined, called and justified us to become conformed to the image of His Son. He also glorified those who are conformed to Jesus' image (see Romans 8:29–30).

When we agree with being equally yoked and aligned with God in the kingdom of the Spirit, we suddenly accelerate, increase or multiply in our evolution toward spiritual maturity. The fire of God will consume the wood, hay and stubble along with the sacrifice of our life that we offer.

It is time for the strength and the beauty of our life to emerge out of the ashes and failures of our past—just like Peter emerged out of the ashes of Simon's failures. In our weakness, Jesus will manifest Himself strong on our behalf. God overshadows us with His goodness, so we can prevail in every situation. God's goodness empowers us to love our enemies as we love ourselves and to overcome evil with the good found in the Fruits of the Spirit.

God's power provides provision, while His revelation knowledge awakens reformation. Therefore, we can ascend to move in a new way. Every problem, no matter what its size, comes with the promise of heavenly provision. *God will supply all of our needs according to the riches of His glory* (Philippians 4:19).

When we use our prophetic words as weapons of warfare, suddenly our problems will flee as we thankfully proclaim the arrival of God's provision. When we obtain the wisdom of God, His goodness announces that our promotion is present! If we want to increase the power of vision, we must give thanks for that which we already possess. A grateful heart celebrates God's goodness and mercy toward us. Giving thanks for All Things brings forth the power of multiplication in our daily life. When we praise, thank and worship God, we become more aware of His increased presence inhabiting our heart.

> *Negativity is a curse that nullifies creativity.*

We have access to heaven's unlimited wisdom, power, authority and resources, but we must believe it is available to us in order to experience it. When the mind consents to a vision as being true, it gives the vision permission to manifest in our waking reality. God wants to awaken us to the infinite multidimensional aspects of who we are in Christ. However, if we fall out of agreement with God's vision for our life, we break the covenant connection or life-sustaining umbilical cord. The vision no longer has a spiritual lifeline that gives it the power to manifest. Without a God-given vision, people perish.

We must remain one with God in spirit and in truth so that the imagination can experience unity. When the imagination is fused with God's point of view, we are tethered to God. We move as one. We are connected to His power to accomplish our God-given purpose and destiny. It is important to learn how to use the imagination properly so that we can discover our purpose and fulfill our destiny. The imagination has the power to connect us with the realm of vision, so we can see how to manifest our desires before our very eyes.

To master the realm of imagination, we should learn how to experience and interpret visions. Manifestation comes when we are able to believe, look and see the final product waiting for us in the future. Then by the faith of God, we enter into the reality of that imaginative realm. By being present in the future, we become partakers of what the vision is showing us by experiencing the end results of the process. If our senses only occasionally entertain a certain concept in our thought or reasoning processes (barely thinking of the concept from time to time), it remains a mere possibility with a large gap between its ability to become a reality.

Goals and destinies are not achieved by merely thinking of them. We must believe it is possible to see it, feel it is already done and develop a strategic plan to capture the prize of the future high calling of God. *Brethren, I do not count myself to have apprehended; but one thing I do, forgetting those things which are behind and reaching forward to those things which are ahead* (Philippians 3:13). If we will immerse ourself in the vision of our desire and apply the Word of God, we can renew our mind. By training ourself to think and see from the end result, we will manifest the creative greatness of Christ who is dwelling within us. Christ is our only hope of obtaining glory.

The imagination is the open double doors that give us access to seeing the reality of Christ living in us. Christ is the only access door to the Father of Glory. The glory realm holds everything we need, want or could ever desire. All of the unlimited riches of Christ are held in reserve for us in the vast domains of glory. As Believers, we learn to access Jesus, who is the spiritual doors of the imagination, so that the things we desire, pray for, hope for and believe for can be seen by faith. The expectations of our desires being realized are then drawn to us. Our desires enter into the natural realm of existence through the gateway of faith.

> *Prophecy humbles us by removing the things of pride in our life that prevents us from trusting God and arising to manifest our future destiny.*

By faith we understand that it is important to think, feel and see beyond our natural senses. The visions we see cause us to verbally decree and prayerfully express the conceptual visions of the things we are hoping for with our spiritual senses. *Now faith is the substance of things hoped for, the evidence of things not seen* (Hebrews 11:1).

God calls things that are not seen as though they were so that the things that are not seen become seen. It is imaginative faith that places our inherent trust and enduring confidence in the power, wisdom and goodness of God. By faith, we begin to understand that the world and the universe we live in were formed, put in order, framed, created and equipped for their intended purposes by the Word of God. That what is seen was not made out of things that are visible.

Never forget God's laws and His spiritual teachings, but write mercy, kindness and every truth you have been given from God upon the tablets of your heart. Leave behind accusations, all deliberate hypocrisy, falsehoods and judgements so you can keep God's commandments. God's favor and good understanding brings the high esteem of man as Christ fashions integrity in your life. His wisdom will add length of days and years of inner tranquility to your life that will continue to satisfy you through old age until the fullness of days.

> *We have access to heaven's unlimited wisdom, power, authority and resources, but we must believe it is available to us in order to experience it.*

Be loyal to love in order to create a reputation of living life well. Place your total confidence in the Lord. Rely on Him, lean on His strong shoulders and trust in His ways with all your heart and mind. Do not rely on your own opinions, natural abilities, limited insights and understandings. Optimism is a skill that is acquired through a lot of daily practice and mental discipline. Never listen to those who tell you it can't be done; that is only their opinion. Dream big, think outside of the box, and imagine yourself doing the impossible. It takes a lifetime to imagine all you are called to do, so keep dreaming and live big. Life is too short to think small.

Let Us Pray

Lord Jesus, help us to take every thought captive by casting down our low self-esteem, victim mentality, the spirit of rejection and the lack of trust in others–along with all of our cynically motivated, destructive strongholds. Show us how to discard all of our negative, fear-based beliefs, anxiety, discouragement, depression, disappointments, doubt and worry. Show us how to identify with You and how to believe Your truths instead of listening to the enemy's destructive lies. Renew our minds by the washing of Your life-giving, creative Word. Give us the keys to access heaven's unlimited wisdom, power, authority and resources. Help us to believe that anything we need is always available to us so that we can experience Your supernatural power manifested in our lives. We ask that You would write Your laws and spiritual teachings upon the tablets of our hearts so that we will never forget them. Help us to place our total trust and confidence in You, Lord. Amen.

CHAPTER TWELVE

Make Room for Change

Believe in God, and He will direct all your ways until you discover the wisdom you need to do the impossible. Recognize God's magnificence. Acknowledge Him in all your ways, and the Holy Spirit will direct you onto the straight, narrow paths to guide your decisions, and you will prosper in all of your ways (see Proverbs 3:1–6).

When we place our faith in God, it will grow as a productive seed of increase and multiplication until we can harvest a greater measure of faith growing into the now faith of God. Faith is NOW! Faith brings a current, present and creative reality that is continually coming to us from out of the Spirit realm. Faith makes it easy to manifest the Kingdom of God in our life.

To emerge with a new identity, our better future self must be awakened, felt, seen, heard and received as a sustainable fact. When we are given a vision of what God intends for us to be, our subconscious instantly imagines us changed into that person. From that moment on, God stops relating to us as the old person. He sees us transformed into our new fullness, having achieved spiritual maturity.

The proceeding Word interacts with us as a different person who carries an additional measure of God's presence, authority and power. A new identity emerges as we now believe and see as God sees. We obediently embrace a different and much larger *God vision* of who we are. A godly identity and vision come with both a promise and its provision. God has provided the creative ideas that form the opportunities to create fresh endowments that will finance our new identity.

God grants us revelation knowledge to bless us and to bless those who are in our sphere of influence. Vision always comes with a strategy to supply in order for prosperity to increase our scope of influence. *Honor the Lord from your wealth and from the first of all your produce; so that your barns will be filled with plenty and your vats will overflow with new wine* (Proverbs 3:9–10).

Once we awaken to our new identity in our imagination, we begin to take on and function in that image in our daily life. Now we are seen as a Son of God who has taken on God's likeness, power and image of splendor. When we agree with God's impressive vision of us, it is instantly written upon the tablets of our heart. Our new, striking image or Christlike identity is made abundantly clear to us. Now we will appear different to the people who knew us before. Our friends and associates who meet us in the future will be amazed at the level of wisdom, spiritual gifting and abilities that we carry. We have become a new creature in Christ.

> *When we place our faith in God, it will grow as a productive seed of increase and multiplication until we can harvest a greater measure of faith growing into the now faith of God.*

When we agree with God, we experience abundance and acceleration. We are given the major kingdom keys that unlock the expanded double doors of access that were previously unobtainable. There are keys to being successful in taking on this new, God-given identity. They are desiring His will, imagining that it is so and focusing our attention on bringing God's Kingdom to earth.

God's manifest presence in our life causes our destiny to be recognized, enlightened, enlarged, magnified and then fulfilled. Proper spiritual alignments and godly agreements cause us to experience multiple opportunities and connections with fantastic, impressive people. These excellent contacts begin to flood in, providing for our increased favor, advancement and overall personal prosperity.

For our faith to bridge the gap between the future (that which is hoped for) and the present (that which currently exists), we must leave the natural reasoning processes in order to cross over into the spiritual dimension of wisdom. The subconscious mind possesses great reservoirs of wisdom that make us aware of godly knowledge. The subconscious helps us know how to apply the power of God in our life so that we live a long, full, all-encompassing and prosperous life.

People grow old when they stop dreaming of conquering innovative ventures in the future. They lose ground when they quit applying themselves by refusing to learn something original. When we draw the curtains and call it a night, sleep overtakes us, and we crawl into bed, pull the covers up over our head, give up, fall asleep and slumber the rest of our life away. Age is not determined by the number of years a person has lived but by the measure of godly wisdom he or she has adopted and assumed in his or her life. For the Believer, the path of life is endless. Life that is found in God carries us from this world into the eternal realms beyond. There, we will never stop learning divine truths.

When we agree with God's impressive vision of us, it is instantly written upon the tablets of our heart.

The Bible makes it clear that there is nothing new under the sun. All Things have already been created and are waiting for us to discover and manifest them in time. *That which has been is what will be, that which is done is what will be done, and there is nothing new under the sun* (Ecclesiastes 1:9).

Our visionary imagination makes us aware of the reality or evidence of something existing beyond the veil. If an image or impression exists but is cloaked in the spiritual realm, it can still be seen, felt, moved and repositioned into another dimension of reality. When we become consciously aware of the existence of our desire, it instantly becomes obtainable.

Faith is the necessary component that empowers Believers to move their invisible desire into a state of being that can be realized in the natural realms of existence.

For, indeed, we have had the glad tidings of the gospel pro-

> *claimed to us, just as truly as they* (the Israelites of old) *did when the good news of deliverance from bondage came to them; but the message they heard did not benefit them, because it was not mixed with faith, with the leaning of the entire personality on God in absolute trust and confidence in His power, wisdom, and goodness by those who heard it; neither were they united in faith with the ones, Joshua and Caleb, who heard and did believe* (Hebrews 4:2).

Biblical principles work for both the saved and the unsaved because they are founded in God's eternal truth. When we exercise faith, it pleases God. Gaining the knowledge found in spiritual insights gives us what we need to fulfill all of our desires.

Our tremendous need for God's wisdom and the ability to obtain all the answers that we need for our prayers already exists in God. Training our faith to seek after the Spirit of Truth makes it easy for us to believe in God. The good news of the gospel makes it possible to mix our faith with the Word of God. Believing in the Word of God makes it possible to obtain all that God has promised us.

God's Intimate Communication

God has given us all of the keys to His Kingdom (as well as the promises in the Word of God) that we need in order to fashion our character in order to reflect Christ's godly image. The Word of God empowers Believers to skillfully mold their life in His likeness.

One of the major avenues the Spirit of God speaks to and shows all of humanity His plans for each person's life is through the imaginative realms of dreams and visions. All of the prophets testify that God continually speaks to them through dreams and visions. *Then He said, "Hear now My words: If there is a prophet among you, I, the Lord, make Myself known to him in a vision; I speak to him in a dream"* (Numbers 12:6).

As I have mentioned in previous volumes, God chooses to use a symbolically-packed spiritual language of pictures to speak to humanity. God combines different symbolic pictures, numbers and colors in various settings to communicate a grand message to us in dreams and visions. A symbol will imprint on our spirit so that we can easily recall it. The symbols God chooses to place together tells an amazing story that speaks a thousand different words to each individual. The symbols in your dreams become a personal dream vocabulary that is a rich, heavenly language; it creates an intimacy to be shared between you and God.

In order to understand the different manners in which God communicates, we need to learn all of His various spiritual enigmas, types, conundrums, myriads of symbols, puns and metaphoric dream languages. To make this process simple and easy, I have compiled thousands of symbols garnered from Scripture and ancient Hebrew interpretation into 160 individually, artistically designed *Dream Symbol Cards* that are also collectively categorized into an amazingly helpful dream interpretation book. Then there is my best-selling *A to Z Dream Symbology Dictionary* that also contains substantial information with over 10,000 unique dream symbols so that dreamers can quickly gain more understanding of their dreams. DreamsDecoder.com is available for those who desire to have master interpreters analyze and reveal the hidden meanings of their dreams.

God's manifest presence in our lives causes our destiny to be recognized, enlightened, enlarged, magnified and then fulfilled.

> *For God may speak in one way, or in another, yet man does not perceive it. In a dream, in a vision of the night, when deep sleep falls upon men, while slumbering on their beds, then He opens the ears of men, and seals their instruction. In order to turn man from his deed, and conceal pride from man* (Job 33:14–17).

We can become anything we desire if we release our faith to see beyond the foundational beginnings of a thing. Looking past your present, current situation or limited qualifications into the next chapter of your life's story, you are able to grow, change and mature. Dreams empower us to evolve into the blessed and skilled individual that God destined for us to become from before the foundations of the world were laid.

Endless Possibilities

Before starting something fresh, we must prayerfully count the cost of a project, relationship or new job venture with the end result in mind. Prayerfully inquire of the Lord, and then consider all of your options. Do not limit yourself to one path. Plan to start building or moving in another direction only after God's wisdom and revelation have been received. Our success is assured when we imagine the future with the end of the matter continually in mind, having already traveled in the Spirit to be in that place of prosperity and having believed, seen and fully known the future outcome.

Imagine what life would be like if you were always successful. Envisioning your success will always empower you to overcome failure on the way to success. If you are open to learning new things, that teachable spirit will ensure you are successful in your personal relationships, marriage or career. Success never happens overnight; it is a lifelong process of being teachable and then teaching others to prosper. Success isn't just about you accomplishing your dreams and life goals. It is more about helping others achieve their own destiny by inspiring them to be great.

> *In order to understand the different manners in which God communicates, we need to learn all of His various spiritual enigmas, types, conundrums, myriads of symbols, puns and metaphoric dream languages.*

The faults that we dislike in others are often evident to us because they also exist within us. It is foolish to find fault in or blame another for our lack. Pointing a critical finger at others who are prejudice or come from a worldly environment or any variety of external circumstances only drains our energy. Criticism doesn't solve anything, but it will definitely stagnate, delay or stop our spiritual growth.

When we pause long enough to take an honest look within, we will see our real condition. If we intently listen to our heart's desire, we will hear our internal language or the self-talk. Our internal voice arises from one of two sources: we either speak out from our negative beliefs or from a positive, creative thought life. Never speak about who you are currently. Talk about who you imagine yourself becoming in the future. May the meditations of my heart or imagination be acceptable to You, Lord! By hearing and observing ourself, we will discover that our own carnal reactions to life's situations are the true reasons for our present condition or tumultuous emotional conflicts.

God gave man a free will in order that we can exercise our stubborn resolve that affords us the ability to find inventive solutions. When we ask, the wisdom of God gives us simple solutions for life's challenges and complicated obstructions. Prayer gives us the answers to any problem by revealing the true reason for any obstacle or set back. With this firsthand knowledge, we have the ability to choose any status in life that we desire. *If you lack wisdom, ask Me, for I will give you an unlimited supply of wisdom so your decisions will be judicious and wise, igniting a continual stream of prosperity and no harm will befall you* (James 1:5).

Let Us Pray

Dear Lord Jesus, we gladly place our faith in You. Help us to discover Your wisdom and recognize Your imposing greatness. Help the seeds of faith that we have sown to grow, increase and multiply until we can harvest a greater measure of faith growing into the now faith of God. Awaken the new identity of our better future selves in order to manifest the Kingdom of God in our lives. Help us to learn how to relate to God in our new, transformed, Christlike image as spiritually mature beings. Grant us revelation knowledge so that we can increase our sphere of kingdom influence. Teach us how to agree with God's plans for our lives so that we will experience an acceleration of wisdom and spiritual abundance. Amen.

CHAPTER THIRTEEN

Imaginative Mansions

Exercising our imagination in a positive manner will help us to establish the Spirit of Christ Jesus operating in our life. Jesus knew how to look into the realm of heaven to see what His Father was doing so that He could mirror God's actions here on earth.

> *Then Jesus answered and said to them, "Most assuredly, I say to you, the Son can do nothing of Himself, but what He sees the Father do; for whatever He does, the Son also does in like manner. For the Father loves the Son, and shows Him All Things that He Himself does; and He will show Him greater works than these, that you may marvel. For as the Father raises the dead and gives life to them, even so the Son gives life to whom He will"* (John 5:19–21).

The Father represents all the multiplied myriads of different states of consciousness that are available to and already prepared for the Believer. The conscious awareness of focused faith has the ability to choose any state of being. Our conscious status can place us in a different state of existence in a higher spiritual house or massive mansion. Different states of consciousness empower us to visit different elegant mansions that are located somewhere in the future.

> *You have heard Me* (conscious) *say to you, "I am going away*

> *and coming back to you. If you loved Me* (Christ-conscious), *you would rejoice because I said, I am going to the Father* (subconscious), *for My Father* (subconscious) *is greater than I* (conscious)*"* (John 14:28).

We can see ourself in a different state of being or visualize another spiritual place even when we know that we are not actually physically there in that place yet. But having visited there in the Spirit, we are able to ascend that same ladder again and again. Soon, we will be able to return to rest in that imaginative state with the keys of faith that are needed to possess that refined mansion, taking on that new identity. We emerge clothed in the attributes and advanced powers, living life as a new creation being.

We believe in God. We also believe in the awareness of IAM, our own conscious existence in God. The conscious mind chooses the state in which we will exist. Then the creative power of the eternal subconscious mind believes the experiences that the conscious mind tells and shows it.

Simply go to sleep believing that you have already received a new state of being. As you persist in that new state, you will awaken conscious of dreaming about experiencing or living in that state. Before falling asleep, ask Christ, who dwells in the subconscious, for an answer to a problem. Upon awakening, you will discover the needed wisdom for the solution. Our spirit man can view all the various rooms, live in the chambers, sleep in the bedrooms and walk down the transitional hallways in this massive house or mansion that is created by God.

> *Exercising our imagination in a positive manner will help us to establish the Spirit of Christ Jesus operating in our life.*

> *In My Father's house are many mansions* (states of consciousness)*; if it were not so, I would have told you. I go to prepare a place for you* (our present state of consciousness ascends and moves into our desired state). *And if I go and prepare a place for you, I will come again* (through answers to prayer, dreams and visions) *and receive you to Myself; that where I am, there you may be also* (John 14:2–3).

Within the walls of this stately mansion, our active thoughts are changed, renewed and guided to a significantly higher concentration of vision where we experience a much broader echelon of the Holy Spirit.

The infinite intelligence of Christ that is found in our subconscious rewards our focused faith with the correct answers to a myriad of diverse situations. The responsive subconscious replies to circumstances with a godly wisdom that solves impossible possibilities. The subconscious holds the power of ingenious creativity for inventions and cures for the incurable, which meet the needs of humanity. All of these amazing dimensional states and diverse gifts await our imagination's discovery. Jesus told us that these mansions exist in the awakened realm of consciousness.

During His earthly ministry, Jesus found it necessary to pray, commune and meditate daily to enter a spiritual state or mansion, to routinely ascend into His Father's presence. The things of the Spirit are always spiritually discerned. We are able to move from one spiritual state of existence of IAM into another state of IAM where we can dwell in a higher degree of God consciousness or enlarged mansion of God.

Different states of consciousness empower us to visit different, elegant mansions that are located somewhere in the future.

The Bible tells us that the Kingdom of God is within us. Therefore, our imagination is able to enter into the Kingdom to alter the future!

> *When the alarms go off in a city people are distressed. God knows when disaster is going to strike. God is the Master of the entire universe yet He does nothing without first declaring the whole truth of His plans to His prophets* (Amos 3:7).

We can believe, see, choose and inhabit the future events that we desire to experience. We can hear the voice of the Holy Spirit telling us about them before they occur on earth. *And now I have told you before it comes, that when it does come to pass, you may believe* (John 14:29).

Jesus related to the world as a flesh and blood human, but He was spiritually connected to His Father in heaven. During Jesus' earthly journey, He was confronted with catastrophic occurrences that were too difficult for Him to handle in His natural strength or state of being. Jesus daily spent time in prayer, sought God's face and went before His heavenly Father's throne to obtain God's counsel. Jesus entered His Father's mansions to receive the divine wisdom and higher levels of spiritual consciousness that He needed. The intimate connection Jesus maintained with His heavenly Father gave Him everything He needed to overcome difficult tests and numerous earthly trails. In these heavenly mansions, Jesus discovered the knowledge He sought in order to do the impossible. *Seek the Lord and His strength; seek His face evermore* (Psalm 105:4)!

Jesus didn't always know how to walk on water, calm a storm or command fish to jump into a net or supply a coin to pay His taxes. Jesus had to learn how to heal the sick and raise the dead. Jesus had to gain spiritual insights and wisdom as He transcended the various heavenly mansions. Jesus continually gained more revelation knowledge by communing in prayer as He dwelt with His heavenly Father in heavenly places or mansions. For us to enter different mansions, rooms, spiritual levels of being or states of consciousness, we also must seek to find the Father.

> *The subconscious holds the power of ingenious creativity for inventions and cures for the incurable, which meet the needs of humanity.*

We can only find the Father through first seeking and finding Jesus. Jesus is the one and only correct door of access. We enter Jesus' presence with the blood of the perfect Lamb of God and with a grateful heart that is full of praise and thanksgiving. We prayerfully ask in faith, continue to diligently knock and then persist in the state of adoration until Jesus (the transformational door) opens. When Jesus hears us knock, He opens the door and invites us to come in to commune and dine with Him. As we enter into His presence, we are transformed into the same image that He is currently displaying for us.

Every dream or vision the Holy Spirit creates within us is an invitation for us to follow the Spirit into the unknown realms of fresh revelation knowledge. The Holy Spirit continually builds us up and constructs, restores or reconstructs us so that we have the ability to enter a different, higher place of revelation knowledge to gain more spiritual understanding. Dreams connect us with the transforming power of the future. *But the fruit of the Spirit is love, joy, peace, long-suffering, kindness, goodness, faithfulness, gentle-*

ness, self-control. Against such there is no law (Galatians 5:22–23).

The present becomes a launching pad that propels us into the future when we are able to release our heartfelt love to God. The Lord's joy comes to strengthen us so that we can rest in God's peace that passes all understanding. By focusing our attention on His gentle kindness, goodness and faithfulness, being still in God's presence, we learn to develop and exercise self-control. In this fashion, we can be what we see in the future and manifest it in our now by resting in that present state.

The state of mind in which we dwell can be a positive ally or friend, but the wrong state of mind, bad attitude or negative thought life or inner voice is an internal foe. *And a man's enemies will be those of his own household* (body, temple, mansion) (Matthew 10:36). Sometimes, we are our own worst enemy.

Jesus came not to bring peace but a sword of truth. This sword is capable of piercing between the soul and spirit. It is a discerner of the thoughts and intents of the heart. We have to war against corrupt ideas that govern bad behavior. Anger creates hostile reactions that try to dominate our mood with depression. We remove the enemies of our soul by repenting and replacing them with positive feelings that produce the right agency of thought. So often, we want the other person to change or stop doing what irritates or annoys us. The only person you have the power to change is yourself. Those who are dead, having never received the free gift of salvation offered to them by Jesus, will be judged according to his works (see Revelation 20:13).

> *Miracles manifest when we learn how faith enters the realm of the Spirit to search out, connect to, transport and then release the Dunamis power into a body or situation.*

Jesus said, "And behold, I am coming quickly, and My reward is with Me, to give to every one according to his work" (Revelation 22:12).

How much life-changing work have you done on yourself? Keep seeking God with all of your heart. When Christ is found of you, you will be like Him. Having already entered into and completed that phase of the transformation process, you are able to fulfill your desire. Continue to hunger and thirst after righteousness so that you will be able to discover a confident, grander model of yourself. Then you will ascend to a higher spiritual level in life. Learn to transcend your present consciousness so that you can conceive something greater in Christ.

Pressing Beyond with the Faith of God

Thomas was known as *Doubting Thomas*. Doubt and unbelief will never carry us anywhere, but it will keep us locked behind the prison gates of fear, which paralyzes us. Fear produces defeat and depression. Is it no wonder Thomas stated, "Lord, we do not know where You are going, and how can we know the way?" If we are not intimate friends with Jesus Christ, we will never know the secrets that give us the keys of the Kingdom of God.

Revelation is a key that unlocks the door. Intimacy empowers us to discover the spiritual mysteries that Jesus freely shares with all of His closest friends. Miracles manifest when we learn how faith enters the realm of the Spirit to search out, connect to, transport and then release the Dunamis power into a body or situation. We gain spiritual understanding to see past the beginning of our current state or present conditions.

Wisdom enables us to obtain the answers that lie at the end of the journey before we reach the end of the road. By seeing through the eyes of faith and believing in our heart, we bring the wisdom of the future into our present state. The wisdom of God changes us and recreates our internal and external environments so that they mirror God's Kingdom on earth.

By seeing through the eyes of faith and believing in our heart, we bring the wisdom of the future into our present state.

God has given us the creative power to translate what we behold in the glory realm of vision by drawing it down into a tangible state of being present on earth. The imagination gives us the creative clarity to translate vision into reality. Remember, occasionally thinking of something only manifests a small amount of faith. If we are a person of little faith, then we are also a person of little power and influence, and we lack any real authority. Without utilizing our full measure of faith, what we have seen in the Spirit is less likely to manifest. But if we learn to consistently think from the manifestation of the final result, then great faith will manifest our vision of hope and fulfill our expectations in its fullness every time.

In heaven, whatever God says is NOW! His commands are instantaneously created, made manifest, released to appear immediately present and are eternally so. There is no time lag or delay, because there is no doubt or unbelief in heaven. We move mountains by animating the faith of God, not by using the limited measure of faith we have in God. The now, present condition that God decrees instantly manifests as reality. Therefore, that which was can also appear in the present, or, if He so desires, something that shall be made manifest in the future (held in reserve to manifest at another time). Faith is the conduit that brings the answers to our prayers out of the waiting room of heaven. Faith ignites the power of God to work on our behalf.

Embracing the Future

The soul can recall the memories of the past. For the soul to prosper, it is necessary to break out of the soul's routine habit of focusing on and rehearsing the past. Your past does not predict your future, so stop accessing it with your memory. Release your spirit to go into the future and create a new door of opportunity. Look to the future, and focus on bringing your full potential back into your present situation.

By renewing or retraining your mind, will and emotions to only look forward into a future hope, not backward into past failures, the positive power of success will erase a negative life script and rewrite a positive life story. That which is past has already been. It is history, yet it still exists, living boldly in your past memories. If you continue to live out of your history, you will repeat the same mistakes. Learn to live out the affirmative, progressive dreams you imagine until they become your reality.

> *God has given us the creative power to translate what we behold in the glory realm of vision into a tangible state of being present on earth.*

Past, present and future events or inventions, future relationships that have not yet formed and the answers to prayer that will come to pass already exist. Yet these forthcoming happenings continue to rest in the unmanifested realms of the future. Coming, imminent opportunities are waiting until we believe, look to see, pray to open the doors of access and decree them into being present in our lives so that we can apprehend them for ourselves. It requires an energetic prayer effort to believe, see, hear and retrieve invitations that beckon to us from the future. And it takes just as much, if not more, effort to dig up and focus upon the painful failures of the past. Learn to invest your energies in the future-present (where your potential will cause the most movement toward prosperity). The past is over, so bury it. The now is present, so live it to its fullest. The future is ahead, so advance into it with all your might in order to bring forth your highest (God-given) expectations into your now.

> *After we have a dream, visionary encounter or experience a visitation, God relates to us as if we have already obtained, retained and become everything that appeared in the dream.*

God knows the end from the beginning, declaring His ingenious thoughts to man (see Amos 4:13). The creative power of God functions from a position of finality. God sees the fulfillment of His desire as an already accomplished miracle, event or end result. God is the Alpha and the Omega, yet He does not stay focused on the beginning. The words of God create the beginning, the in-betweens, the middle and a glorious, final conclusion. God lives in eternity, yet He looks ahead into the future and focuses on the completed results. The creative powers of the Spirit realm move at an accelerated rate.

Jesus knew each of us before we were conceived in our mother's womb. He planned all of our days from the first to the last. He knew the purposes and plans that He designed for us to fulfill. He knew the decisions we would make before we were even born. He skillfully placed the gifts and knowledge within that we would need to navigate the diverse paths and to manifest the different states of being in life.

> *Jesus responded, "Every scholar of the Scriptures, who is instructed in the ways of heaven's kingdom realm, is like a wealthy home owner with his house filled with treasures both new and old. And he knows how and when to bring them out to display and show others"* (Matthew 13:52).

After we have a dream, visionary encounter or experience a visitation, God relates to us as if we have already obtained, retained and become everything that appeared in the dream. He thinks of and relates to us as if we are already mature in Christ (having apprehended every one of our life goals) because it is now so in the Spirit. We must learn to activate our imagination to consciously think and feel the emotions that we experienced from obtaining the manifestation of the end results.

In order to enter into a new and higher state of being or mansion, we must stay focused on reaching and maintaining the prize. Nothing is accomplished when we only occasionally think of something that we desire. That which is currently present and seeable has already been manifested from before the foundation of the world.

Let Us Pray

Father God, we humbly seek Your face for the wisdom that will forever change us by bringing us into our future state of being. Teach us how to use the creative power of our imagination so that we can translate and decode vision into reality. Empower us to use the full measure of the faith that You have given us. Help us to break our soul out of its routine habits in order to experience Your glory in a new reality. Help us to bury the past, experience the now and pray in the future fullness of our destiny. Amen.

CHAPTER FOURTEEN

Glory Clouds

As we humble ourselves and pray, we submit our will to God's plans and purposes. Humility causes us to access the mercy of God. Honoring both God and man empowers us to obtain wisdom that causes us to prosper in His glory. God clothes Himself in the weighty clouds of Kabod glory, in a cloudy garment of light and thick darkness that conceals His majestic face from our sight. God remains concealed, hidden in mystery, until we learn to seek to find Him with all of our heart. Worshipping God in spirit and truth will reveal Him to us.

Sometimes dark clouds can represent a gloomy time of difficulty or trouble, and they can cause feelings of depression, confusion or heaviness. They can be an indication of lack of vision, or they can be a sign of spiritual warfare, obstacles or possibly something coming against one's reputation. Dark clouds descend, surround and clothe us in gloom and misery when we accept or entertain a negative state of hopelessness, self-pity or despair. The lack of revealed spiritual knowledge is a characteristic of spiritual death, because it comes from the soulish realm or the Tree of the Knowledge of Good and Evil.

The apostles and prophets of God reveal spiritual knowledge. They release spiritual warfare by exercising their authority and revealing the supernatural power of God for breakthrough of deliverance from demons, sickness and disease.

To change a negative, dark state of consciousness, we must stop focusing our conscious thoughts on a miserable, low state of existence. Like Moses, who God used to deliver a nation, we must draw out the creative power of Christ's presence that dwells within us by igniting the fiery pillar of God's powerful light of truth.

> *Take careful heed to yourselves, for you saw no form when the Lord spoke to you at Horeb out of the midst of the fire, lest you act corruptly and make for yourselves a carved image in the form of any figure* (Deuteronomy 4:15–16).

Have you ever rested on your back in a beautiful field of green grass just to look up at the fluffy, white clouds billowing by? It's fun to use our imagination to see all of the different cloud creatures that appear and float past. Clouds are also a symbol of God's divine guidance, wisdom and supernatural covering that gives us oversight and the provision that is necessary to shade us by day. Clouds move, cover, hover, descend, refresh, lift and ascend.

The individual droplets of water within clouds converge, connect and unite to form God's covenant rainbows and raindrops. Clouds pour out rain. Rain represents: God's blessings; refreshing; replenishing; cleansing; an outpouring or shower of the Spirit or Word of God; spiritual teaching; abundance of praise; or to shower with compliments. When these raindrops converge, connect and unite, they form a stream and fill wells that spring up, flow and overflow. The overflowing presence of God forms rivers that will never run dry but will water all the barren places.

To change a negative, dark state of consciousness, we must stop focusing our conscious thoughts on a miserable, low state of existence.

Clouds move in different directions as the Spirit leads. When we embrace a higher level of spiritual truth, clouds are blown by the Spirit's wind to lift up or ascend. Clouds move and shift when atmospheres change. Clouds fill in every empty space and take on different foggy forms and images. We change heavenly atmospheres, geographic states or our personal states of being through prayer, decreeing and declaring the Word of God, through giving testimonies and through praising and worshiping God.

The presence of God clothes us in those same clouds of glory as we learn to change the states of our being. We rise from one level of glory to the next, higher dimension of wisdom, light and glory. Because today's Believers are born again of God's Spirit, they are qualified for a far deeper, more personal encounter with God than Moses was. *And the Lord spoke to you out of the midst of the fire. You heard the sound of the words, but saw no form; you only heard a voice* (Deuteronomy 4:12).

In Exodus, Israel chose to look at a cloud that appeared like a consuming fire from afar. The people of Israel chose to keep their distance and stay away from God's transforming fire, unlike Moses who eagerly entered God's glory cloud of encounter. Like a moth drawn into the fire, Moses desired to be totally consumed by God. The people of Israel were directed by the presence of a cloud of glory by day and a pillar of glory fire by night. Sadly, the people of Israel never entered into the glory of the holy place themselves.

The presence of God clothes us in those same clouds of glory as we learn to change the states of our being.

> *The Lord our God made a covenant with us in Horeb. The Lord did not make this covenant with our fathers, but with us, those who are here today, all of us who are alive. The Lord talked with you face to face on the mountain from the midst of the fire. I stood between the Lord and you at that time, to declare to you the Word of the Lord; for you were afraid because of the fire, and you did not go up the mountain* (Deuteronomy 5:2–5).

The level of our visionary capacity that determines our ability to believe and see God depends upon the degree that we have removed idolatry from our heart. Jesus warned that in the last days, in which we now live, people will be lovers of self and completely self-centered. They will be lovers of money who are aroused by an inordinate greed that desires wealth at any cost. They will seek to take money from the wealthy and redistribute it to the poor. They will be proud and arrogant, a contemptuous, scrupulous bunch of boasters who will break in and steal whatever they want. They will be blasphemous, scoffing against God, and they will be abusive toward women, disobedient to parents, ungrateful, unholy and profane (see 2 Timothy 3:2). *But the Lord is good. He is a refuge in times of trouble. He takes care of those who trust in Him* (Nahum 1:7).

Believers are a chosen, special people—a royal priesthood, a dedicated nation—purchased by God to show forth and display His wonderful deeds, virtues and perfection. He called us out of darkness into His wonderful, marvelous kingdom light (see 1 Peter 2:9). It is essential to refine, elevate and concentrate our focus on God in order to experience His resident and over-shadowing presence.

God can only be seen through the belief in Jesus Christ. Do not reduce God to a formula based on the principles and traditions practiced by others. Instead, constantly develop your own personal, intimate relationship with the Christ that dwells within. We do not see or experience the blessings or benefits of the revelation of Christ's presence unless we first seek the Kingdom of God. By entering into His presence and gazing upon His beautiful face, we make Christ our reigning King. *"And I will not hide My face* (in the cloud) *from them anymore; for I shall have poured out My Spirit on the house of Israel," says the Lord God* (Ezekiel 39:29).

> The level of our visionary capacity that determines our ability to see God depends upon the degree that we have removed idolatry from our heart.

We should strive to incessantly seek to find the hidden face of God. My book *DREAM SEER: Searching for the Face of the Invisible* will give you the revelation knowledge needed to manifest and behold the beautiful countenance of Jesus. The manifestations of God's presence appear through a still, small voice, a gentle touch, a breeze, the brush of an angel's wing or a mighty rushing wind. The manifestations of His presence appear through the glow of the moon, the shining of the sun and the brightness of countless galaxies of stars. They also appear through dreams, visions, amazing signs, wonders and miracles.

> *"And it shall come to pass in the last days," says God, "That I will pour out of My Spirit on all flesh; your sons and your daughters shall prophesy, your young men shall see visions, your old men shall dream dreams. And on My menservants and*

> *on My maidservants, I will pour out My Spirit in those days; and they shall prophesy. I will show wonders in heaven above and signs in the earth beneath: blood and fire and vapor of smoke. The sun shall be turned into darkness, and the moon into blood, before the coming of the great and awesome day of the Lord. And it shall come to pass that whoever calls on the name of the Lord shall be saved"* (Acts 2:17–21; see Joel 2).

Almighty God, who spoke the universe into being, dwells within us; therefore, we are the most blessed generation in history. We are experiencing the indwelling presence of God that is also combined with the outpouring of both the early and the latter presence of God's rain. *For it is the God who commanded light to shine out of darkness, who has shone in our hearts to give the light of the knowledge of the glory of God in the face of Jesus Christ* (2 Corinthians 4:6).

Father God is a good father who knows how to give good and perfect gifts to His children. *Every good gift and every perfect gift is from above, and comes down from the Father of lights, with whom there is no variation or shadow of turning* (James 1:17). The measure of God's light that we feel, hear, see, taste, receive and obey makes our consciousness aware of the degree of power and indwelling presence of God's greatness that is alive within us.

Our consciousness is made up of all that we desire, seek, love and believe is true. Before an individual can positively impact the world, he or she must become God-conscious. When the mind is transformed by the renewing Word of God, we are able to think God thoughts that can convert lives, shift atmospheres and change the circumstances that surround us.

Experiencing God's Glory

The Holy Spirit is waiting for us to awaken our imagination to recognize His majestic, abiding presence. The Holy Spirit manifests His visions for life, His creative ideas and the healing power that Christ is constantly projecting to us through our imagination. Every time we discover another dimension of God's fullness, which has always been there dwelling within us, we are given permission to manifest that idea or form of His powerful presence in and through our life. *For He whom God has sent speaks the words of God, for God does not give the Spirit by measure* (John 3:34). The godly beliefs that we hold as true today will continue to form our inner vision, and they will create virtue within our character.

We put faith into active practice by believing that we already are what we behold in spiritual visions of the future and by adopting that vision as a present reality and personal truth. By placing our faith in God, we are able to grow to attain to the full stature or measure of greatness that God predestined for us in order to manifest the faith of God. When we believe that we are already different, we will stop accepting our same old reactions. We will crucify the old man of guilt and shame. Sin, guilt and shame will fade away as they lose their hold on us. In the place of shame, God's love, compassion and dignity come forth as we are resurrected as a new person with a new identity in Christ.

The progressive Word of God comes to open the spiritual eyes of our understanding so that we can see. His wisdom comes to show us how to be changed into His image. *And they were not able to resist the wisdom and the Spirit by which he spoke* (Acts 6:10). Once the Spirit of God comes to enlighten us, we break out of the limited perceptions of God that we presently hold. For the first time, we realize the unlimited possibilities that await us when we receive the grace to take on the divine nature of God in the realm of faith.

The gifts, anointings and talents that dwell within us cannot be realized or applied in our individual lives if we do not receive them as an absolute truth that has become a real active part of us.

Personal Reflection Moment

Self-deprecation is a destructive practice; it defeats us by dismantling our gifts, abilities or whatever positive things we believe about ourself.

1. Do you fully love and accept yourself?
2. If not fully, then what aspects do you not?
3. What type of attitudes do you display about yourself?
4. What attitudes do you have toward others?
5. Are you willing to imagine yourself in a different way?
6. Can you imagine yourself being seen in a more fa-

vorable, broader, brighter spotlight? If not, you will always remain the same.

Proverbs 23:7 states: *As a man thinks about himself in his heart* (imagination), *so is he.* Therefore, we must guard the thoughts of our heart and focus on discovering, developing and manifesting the IAM portion of that which we are in God. We do this by placing the reality of the living Christ dwelling in us at the control center of our whole being.

If we falsely believe that people—the media, family members, (especially mothers or fathers), friends, peers or associates combined with any other type of outside influences—can determine the state of our being or the conditions that manifest in our life, we have already relinquished over to another the power we once held to make our own decisions. In dream events, the manifestation of this will appear as someone else driving and making all the decisions in the driver's seat of your vehicle. You are in the passenger seat or, worse yet, in the backseat being taken for a ride to a place where you have no input and no control.

It is essential to refine, elevate and concentrate our focus on God in order to experience His resident and over-shadowing presence.

God wants to be the CEO in charge of designing, framing and creating your highest destiny. You must determine what you want out of life. Are you going to allow family members who are so familiar to you or other outsiders who see your limitations determine your potential or who you will be? You must decide to let your imagination rule your world in order to reach your potential.

You prevent your own positive changes when you surrender your ability to make your own decisions—when you willingly take on the limitations imposed on you by others. Strive to be like courageous Caleb who confidently declared before all the people, *Let us go up at once, and possess it; for we are well able to overcome it* (Numbers 13:30). Stop giving someone else the power to form, rule, dictate or critique your life. The only opinion that really matters is yours in agreement with God's. He says you are loved! You are accepted in the Beloved! You are fearfully and wonderfully made! You are altogether lovely in the eyes of God!

God possesses the entire blueprint for the imagination. When we see and act upon the concepts that Christ projects on our image center, we are energized to become that ideal person that we have beheld. This newly imagined person would instantly take us far beyond the natural sphere of our development. Declare to God:

> *Oh, yes, you shaped me first inside then out; You formed me in my mother's womb. I thank you, High God—you're breathtaking! Body and soul, I am marvelously made! I worship in adoration—what a creation! You know me inside and out. You know every bone in my body. You know exactly how I was made, bit-by-bit, how I was sculpted from nothing into something. Like an open book, God You watched me grow from conception to birth; all the stages of my life were spread out before You, the days of my life all prepared before I'd even lived one day* (Psalm 139:14–16).

The world around us continually adjusts in order to agree with our current attitudes and self-concepts. To change our life events or to go in a certain direction, we must transform the current beliefs of our mind. By adopting the godly principles found in the Word of God, we are transformed into a new creature that is inhabited by Christ. The creative Word of God remolds our attitudes so that they can evolve into a higher creative order. This elevated image will be a healthier conceptualization of our new, happy and content self.

Redemption comes through seeing yourself in a vastly different manner. Regardless of whatever was lost, omitted, stolen or diseased, you must begin to see it restored back to you—redeemed, healed, revitalized, increased, whole and multiplied. God restores us from the brink of death, and He revives our life by opening new pathways for us to experience the pleasures of His amazing presence. The Holy Spirit leads our feet upon righteous paths to bring honor to the name of Jesus.

If we are currently experiencing poor health, we must apply the creative, delivering and healing words of God. Declare, "IAM healed in the name of Jesus!" Now, "Let the weak say, 'IAM strong!'"

Decreeing and believing the Word of God releases the healing power within us. The Word of God changes a negative concept we hold of ourself into a positive realization of God's miracle-working power manifesting in our life. God's desire for us is that we prosper and be in good health while the imagination of our mind, our will and our emotions also prosper. *Beloved, I pray that you may prosper in All Things and be in health, just as your soul prospers* (3 John 1:2). This declaration of prosperity must be received as our personal truth and desire.

Our inner voice, independent will and personal belief systems must all agree with and echo the internal voice of God's speech. Christ said, *I have come that you may have life, and that they may have it more abundantly* (John 10:10). Are you living the abundant life? God's abundance is waiting for you to step into the mansion of above and take up residence in the beyond, to live in the place of fullness and more than enough.

The Spirit of Christ dwelling within us communicates with us by accessing the creative, inspirational vehicle of our imagination. The imagination has the power to hear, see, envision and create a path for an evil life or a godly, affluent future. Inspiration will spark the imagination. The free spirit of the imagination will carve out a path of gold wherever it is free to roam.

In seeing through the eyes of God, we learn to believe that All Things are possible! In believing that we can develop a plan to prophesy, pray and decree God's spiritual strategies into existence, we skillfully acquire every desire.

> *We put faith into active practice by believing that we already are what we behold in spiritual visions of the future and by adopting that vision as a present reality and personal truth.*

Prayer is a spiritual force that creates a new reality by first forgiving you. Then we must forgive the misdeeds, hurtful words and sin of all men. Our forgiveness has the power to heal and deliver us. Our forgiveness releases people of their wrongful thoughts, beliefs, actions, deeds and expressions. Mercy and compassion open a new doorway on a higher path of purity that leads to acquiring clean hands and a pure heart (imagination) of holiness.

The imagination empowers us to see the visions of God. Visions come so that we can develop a strategic plan. Visions show us how to know and attain our next level of revelatory directives given by God to fulfill our purposes. The God-given decisions we make set us on a positive course that triggers the domino effect of growth and success. As we continue to ask God for wisdom, seek His face and knock on new doors, we will continue to gain access keys to a more prosperous life.

The purposes we fulfill in life help us to wisely choose the grandest of our grand destinies. As we humble ourselves to ascend into the further dimension of the reverential fear of the Lord, there are a myriad of choices we have to make. *For the Lord giveth preeminent, skillful godly wisdom: out of His mouth comes instruction, knowledge and understanding* (Proverbs 2:6). Each correct choice determines the availability of the next higher rung of now prosperity that we can ascend heavenward on the spiritual ladder of success. As we continue to climb up the vertical ladder of success, we gain access to the Father's heart and His many mansions and vast estates.

The wisdom of God gives us the power to explore these dimensionally diverse mansions. The longer we are able to sustain these higher levels of thoughts, images and actions, the quicker we are transformed and assimilated into them. Our prayerful, focused attention causes us to take on their nature, characteristics and attributes to become them, mirroring and exuding their power.

The Spirit of Christ dwelling within us communicates with us by accessing the creative, inspirational vehicle of our imagination.

We are transformed as we come and go, ascend and descend, live and move and have our sustained being in Christ. We grow in wisdom and take on the dimensional attributes of the mansions that we have inhabited. By being renewed in the power of our mind, we become higher spiritual beings.

The God of the heavens has appointed us for His purposes. He gives us His grace, peace and all that He has to ensure our success. The ultimate purpose of man is to know and worship God. Our imagination empowers us to see and experience Jesus, to forgive sins and to pursue our highest destiny in Christ. The Father says, "You are forever and always with Me and all that I have is thine" (see Luke 15:31).

God keeps us occupied and focused on the joy of His heart. When the tranquility of God indwells us, He causes us to arise and thrive. Holy Spirit records all of our sacrificial giving and spiritual disciplines so that He can build our mansions, decorating them with precious, living stones and furnishing their massive rooms with everything our heart desires.

Let Us Pray

Lord, we humble ourselves and pray so that we can access Your great mercies. We honor You, God, and willingly submit our will to Your perfect plans and purposes. Please empower us to obtain the godly wisdom that is necessary to cause us to prosper in Your glory. Thank you for the good and perfect gifts that You have given to each of us. Teach us how to feel, hear, see and taste Your goodness every day. Transform our minds by the renewing Word so that we can think God thoughts that will convert our lives, shift atmospheres and change circumstances around us. Awaken our imaginations to recognize and see Your majestic, abiding presence. Amen.

CHAPTER FIFTEEN

Beholding the Kingdom

Through the proper development of our imagination, we have the ability to see how to enter into God's presence. God consciousness empowers the Holy Spirit to reveal secrets hidden in mysteries so that we can outwardly manifest the power of the Kingdom of God that dwells within us.

Jesus replied to Nicodemus, "Very truly I tell you, no one can see the Kingdom of God unless they are born again" (John 3:3). Nicodemus represents the priesthood, but He does not understand simple spiritual concepts. Jesus was encouraging Nicodemus to leave his present self-concepts behind and to let go of his religious expressions so that he could embrace a relationship with the living Savior.

Jesus spoke an eternal truth to Nicodemus, a respected teacher in Israel. Jesus stated that Nicodemus must be born from above. *Jesus answered, "Very truly I tell you, no one can enter the kingdom of God unless they are born of water and the Spirit"* (John 3:5). Unless you are born of water, the Word and the Spirit, you will never be able to enter God's Kingdom. The natural, earthly realm only gives birth to the natural.

The spiritual, heavenly realm gives birth to the divine, supernatural wind of the Spirit that blows within where it chooses. *For the Kingdom of God is not a matter of talk but of power* (1 Corinthians 4:20). Believers who have both seen and learned how to consciously enter into the Kingdom of God move in great power and authority.

You can hear the sound of the wind, but you do not know from where it came or where it is going. Jesus spoke eternal truths about heaven by using the natural things He knew and saw on earth. Jesus had the mysteries and wisdom of the Kingdom that were concealed in His Father's heart revealed to Him through imaginative prayer.

> *And My heavenly Father Who sent Me is ever with Me; My Father has not left Me alone, for I always do what pleases Him. I tell you the truth about the things which I have seen and learned at My Father's side* (John 8:38).

Jesus shared what He had seen, heard and experienced in heavenly realms with Nicodemus, but the Rabbi did not understand the revelation. *Jesus said, "The knowledge of the secrets of the Kingdom of God has been given to you, but to others I speak in parables so that, though seeing, they may not see; though hearing, they may not understand"* (Luke 8:10).

Jesus questioned Nicodemus by asking, "If you are not able to believe or understand these earthly, natural things, how can I share heavenly revelation with you?" The Bible tells us that no man has risen into the heavenly realms, except the Son of Man (who is bilocated in the multi-dimensional mansions of the heavens while He is also on earth).

> Through the proper development of our imagination, we have the ability to see how to enter into God's presence.

Spiritual sight opens the eyes of our heart to see who God had already empowered us to become from before the foundations of the earth. Nothing is impossible with God, so we can become anything or anyone that God desires for us to be.

Christ dwells within us, so we are not dependent upon any outside forces. Faith in God causes us to believe in the power of the indwelling Christ who now fills our reality. When we believe that the power of Christ in us gives us the ability to do All Things, His presence causes us to enlarge, prosper and succeed. Christ Jesus living within us is our unlimited inner source. We are not our source of supply. Education, other people, family, government, money, work or any other form of commerce are not our sources of supply.

But seek first the Kingdom of God and the righteousness that proceeds from Him, and all these other things that you have need of shall be added to you in abundance (Matthew 6:33). The proper use of the imagination can create spiritual, emotional and physical wealth beyond anything we have ever experienced before. The unlimited imagination is the womb that stretches until it births the expanses of an obtainable reality.

Our imagination has the power to animate ideas, change the world we live in, resurrect things we have forgotten, kill negative thoughts and actions and generate unlimited realms of possibilities. God's desire is that we prosper and be in health as our soul prospers. The soul is housed within our physical body. The wealth and prosperity that God desires for us to discover is already contained within the expansive reserves found resting in the imagination of our mind, will and emotions. *Wealth and riches will be in his house, and his righteousness endures forever* (Psalm 112:3).

Every good and perfect gift comes down to man from the Father of Lights. God has given mankind spiritual gifts, riches, possessions and honor, so we lack nothing for our soul of all that we might desire (see Ecclesiastes 6:2).

When we lay hands on others to give of the spiritual gifts that we have been given, it also stirs up the gifts that they (others) have been given. Our generous spirit of giving to help others also causes their anointing to come back to us. When they and we collectively add together our good measures, our gifts are pressed down and shaken together. The mingling of our gifts rise up to a new level of blessing that runs over. For with the measure of love that we use to deal out, impart to and confer benefits on (or resurrect gifts in) other people, it will be measured back to us (see Luke 6:38).

> *God consciousness empowers the Holy Spirit to reveal secrets hidden in mysteries so that we can outwardly manifest the power of the Kingdom of God that dwells within us.*

God's gifts and His callings are irrevocable. He never withdraws them once they are given, and He does not change His mind about those to whom He gives His grace or to whom He sends His call (see Romans 11:29).

Having gifts, faculties, talents or qualities that differ according to the grace given us, let us awaken them, resurrect, steward and learn how to use them. He who has a vocal gift to speak, let him or her prophesy according to the proportion of his or her faith (Romans 12:6).

We have not received a spirit that belongs to the world; we have received the Holy Spirit. The Holy Spirit is given to us that we might impart resurrection power into people. This life-giving power ignites the dormant gifts that have always been within each individual Believer, so they can realize, comprehend and appreciate the gifts of divine favor and blessing that God has so freely and lavishly bestowed on them (see 1 Corinthians 2:12).

If I conjure up harmful imaginations of doubt and fear that someone hates me or wants to cause me harm, is jealous of me or is against me, and if I receive the planting of these destructive seeds and believe and water them, each harmful impression will in pregnant me with a plague-ridden crop of (real) horrible images. If I continue to develop and birth these lethal ideas, they hold the power to deliver their negative expressions and spew deadly poison into my world. *Death and life are in the power of the tongue, and those who love it will eat its fruit* (Proverbs 18:21).

> Spiritual sight opens the eyes of our heart to see who God had already empowered us to become from before the foundations of the earth.

We have choices. Poor decisions funnel us into a downward spiral that leads to failure. Doubt opens a trapdoor that instills the grip of carnal fear, which imprisons us in the natural, earthly realm of unbelief.

Personal Reflection Moment

1. God has created us as speaking spirits who have been given the power to make wise choices in life. What does your imagination conjure on a regular basis? And is it authentic or accurate?
2. You may wonder, "Why has my imagination created these self-defeating, vain imaginations?" *See, I have*

set before you today life and good, death and evil (Deuteronomy 30:15).

3. Take a moment to consider what you imagine and the thoughts you entertain. Are they life-giving? Or are they harmful imaginations and thoughts of doubt and fear?
4. If so, you may wonder, "Why am I receiving fear, doubt and death instead of life-giving faith?"

I call heaven and earth as witnesses today against you, that I have set before you, life and death, blessing and cursing; therefore, choose life, that both you and your descendants may live (Deuteronomy 30:19).

The choices we make today not only affect us but also (positively or negatively) affect others and future generations. Jesus, our fundamental leader, said, "IAM the way!" A true spiritual leader is one who knows the *Way* and goes the way of Jesus. When we have become a leader, success is achieved when we invest in others to become successful leaders. We become our true self when we become a leader. The greatest leaders are not ones who accomplish the greatest things. The greatest leaders are those who inspire others to become great in Christ.

Believing that we have already received the revelation of how to run our own life, family, corporation, ministry, business or how to utilize a powerful gift or new aspect of our identity that was demonstrated or seen in the end result causes it to become a personal truth and reality. Embracing and possessing the end result that has been waiting for our discovery cause it to become a NOW (actual) event that was always meant for us to obtain and experience.

To advance spiritually, we must review the visions and dreams the Spirit of God has implanted or shown us in our imagination.

The increase and prosperity demonstrated in the vision of the end result will manifest within us when we decide to incorporate their attributes as truthful statements, points of reference or happenings that flow into our spirit and are adopted as new life patterns. To bring in the different possibilities, higher thoughts and better options that are available to us, we have to clear out the old ways of thinking and doing things. The removal of the outdated makes room for the innovative, new and extraordinary manifestations of the imagination.

Let Us Pray

Holy Spirit, we ask that You would reveal to us the secrets of God that have been hidden in mysteries. Give us the wisdom, spiritual understanding and power that are essential for us to see the Kingdom of God that dwells within us. We believe that the power of the indwelling Christ gives us the ability to do All Things. Help us to seek the Kingdom of God first in all that we say and do. Amen.

CHAPTER SIXTEEN

A Call to Destiny

The biblical story of a Hadassah orphan, who became a celebrated queen, is an exceptional paradigm of one who chose to press past thoughts of fear and doubt to constructively change the dire fate of her people. Can you imagine what type of imaginative transformation had to take place for a lowly, captive, orphaned Jewish girl to rise to the highest position a woman could obtain in a male-dominated Persian country? And can you imagine the faith and perseverance it took to not relent in doubt or shrink back in fear?

In those days, females did not attend school to be educated. Hadassah (Esther) was adopted, raised and educated by her uncle, Mordecai. Esther was born to Mordecai's uncle, yet he raised her as his own daughter. *The maiden was beautiful, fair and lovely, and when her father and mother died, Mordecai, an attendant in the King's court, took her as his own daughter* (Esther 2:7).

When Queen Vashti refused to entertain King Ahasuerus' guests, she was exiled. The king ordered all of the beautiful virgins of his land to be brought to the palace so that he could choose a new queen. Esther went through extended months of beauty treatments, preparation and training. Esther, with her primo genes, her love for academics, her genius, problem-solving Jewish mind and her beautiful, grace-filled countenance, won favor with all who saw her. Esther was chosen above all of the other virgins to become the new Persian queen. Esther had the whole package. She was a perfect

10 plus!

Because Mordecai would not bow to worship Haman (a vizier in the Persian Empire), reverence his position or give him honor, Haman hated the Jews. So Haman sought to destroy the whole Jewish nation. Esther chose to fast and pray prior to going before the king to ask for the lives of her people. She had kept her Jewish heritage a secret. If the king did not extend his scepter when Esther entered the court, she would be executed. She was willing to sacrifice her life to save her people. She took the stance, "If I perish, I perish. But God has placed me here in this elevated government position for such a time as this!"

Esther prepared a banquet for the king and her honored guest and enemy, Haman. There, in the presence of the king, she exposed Haman's evil plot to destroy her and all of her people. A new decree was written by Esther and Mordecai so that the Jews could fight and protect their lives and property.

Haman and his sons were hung on the very gallows he had built to murder Mordecai. Thereafter, Esther set Mordecai over the house of Haman. Because the fear of Mordecai had fallen upon them, all of the princes of the provinces, chief rulers, governors and all those who attended to the king's business helped the Jews. Mordecai became great in the king's palace. His fame went forth throughout all the provinces, for Mordecai became more and more powerful.

> *Doubt and fear are two of our greatest enemies; they produce failure and dis-ease within the thoughts of our own mind.*

Think of all the high achievers, world changers and Jewish Nobel Prize winners (like Albert Einstein) who were rewarded for their innovative inventions that have changed the world for the better. A few mentionable ones are the drip irrigation, the rooftop solar heat water system, laser projection keyboards and the Iron Dome rocket interception system. Think of all of the advanced mathematic formulations, breakthroughs in chemistry and physics and medical cures that have been given to the world through the Jewish nation. None of these things would exist today if Esther had not chosen to place her own life on the line for the nation of Israel. If Esther had not successfully fulfilled her destiny, the Jewish people would have been wiped off the face of the earth. The choices that we make do influence, affect and change the world.

We all have our individual destiny that somehow intertwines with one another; it is God's great design. God is calling each of us to rise up and behold our destiny for such a time as this! We must see what the Father is doing in our life and what He is doing in our lives collectively as Believers, and we must join Him and fulfill all that He has purposed for each and every one of us.

Reaping What We've Sown

Have you ever asked yourself why you are not a Nobel Prize-winning world changer? Is it possibly because negative projections are manifesting in your life?

In due season, we will reap a harvest of whatever we have sown. Whether we are blessed or cursed depends on whether we have sown the field with good seeds or wicked seeds. When we plant seeds that will yield godly purposes, we will reap a harvest of increased blessings, fruits of creativity, wealth, health and life-giving power. But we must also remember what the Word of God warns:

> *Do not be deceived, God is not mocked; for whatever a man sows, that he will also reap. For he who sows to his flesh will of the flesh reap corruption, but he who sows to the Spirit will of the Spirit reap everlasting life. And let us not grow weary while doing good, for in due season we shall reap if we do not lose heart* (Galatians 6:7–9).

Doubt and fear are two of our greatest enemies. They produce failure and dis-ease within the thoughts of our own mind. To change a spiraling, toxic condition, we must turn inside to open and search out what resides within the heart.

> *When we realize the intensity of our own shortcomings, we are more apt to receive and offer God's great grace to overlook or cover others' flaws.*

> *Sow for yourselves righteousness; reap in mercy; break up your*

> *fallow ground, for it is time to seek the Lord, till He comes and rains righteousness on you. You have plowed wickedness; you have reaped iniquity. You have eaten the fruit of lies, because you trusted in your own way, in the multitude of your mighty men* (Hosea 10:12–13).

When negative, hateful, critical or judgmental images arise upon the screens of our imagination, it is time to repent and do some self-reflecting and house cleaning. *They sow the wind and reap the whirlwind. The stalk has no bud; it shall never produce meal. If it should produce, aliens would swallow it up* (Hosea 8:7).

Personal Reflection Moment

1. Consider asking yourself if you have damaged, cursed or hurt someone by binding them with unkind, critical or controlling words. *Even as I have seen, those who plow iniquity and sow trouble reap the same* (Job 4:8).
2. You may want to ask yourself, "Am I being selfish, dominating, manipulative or fearful?" *Those who sow in tears shall reap in joy* (Psalm 126:5).
3. Are you responding to someone or something in a harsh, judgmental manner?
4. Do you criticize others instead of relating to them through thoughts of grace and love? *He who observes the wind will not sow, and he who regards the clouds will not reap* (Ecclesiastes 11:4).
5. What lie do you believe or confess about others or yourself?
6. Are you critical of or think hate-filled thoughts about others or yourself?

   To affect change in our unlovely life situations or circumstances, we must first determine the reason for the negative root.

Quit agreeing with All Things that are false or harmful! It is impossible for change to occur while we continue to entertain the destructive thoughts that keep us stagnant. Renounce what is impeding your victory. Stop focusing your attention on the problem. Close the door to the trauma, and reject the hurt. See yourself obtaining the virtue to become the solution to every problem. Focus on being the answer, not on the reality of the difficulty.

The former mountainous state of being passes away quickly when we focus on the kingdom solution within us. Now is the accepted time for our faith to release the consciousness of the kingdom of heaven that has been established in the earthen heart of our being.

After you have repented, rebuked and uprooted all hindrances, ask God for healing and restoration. Be willing to completely let go of the past, exchanging wrong beliefs with present truth. Replace the former negative, damaging thoughts and feelings with a positive Scripture. Form a creative, life-giving belief that exists in the higher God-conscious realm of understanding. It is necessary that you learn how to speedily return to Christ consciousness in order to release Christ's loving thoughts of grace and mercy unto yourself and others.

If we retain a conscious awareness of any wrong we have suffered at the hands of another, we bind ourselves to them.

The thoughts we think contain a creative power. We often to do not take into consideration the weight of this power we hold. People can spiritually perceive and receive our thoughts toward them. Once people perceive our judgments toward them, they are mentally recorded, recalled and retained by them as memories. The shoe can also be on the other foot. Have you ever perceived another's thoughts or judgements toward you, although no words were spoken to confirm or deny those perceptions? Being acutely aware of this creative power assists us in yielding it with great caution.

By sowing love, we free people from their limitations. They are delivered from the captivity that we have projected onto them from our negative thoughts about and caustic actions toward them. When our conscious thoughts of them change, the former things have passed away. Only the power of love can wholly heal the adverse perceptions we have had about others. Only the power of love can counteract the negative ways we have consistently reacted toward certain, troubling people.

Are you aware that the injurious character traits, irritating behaviors, negative patterns or the frustrating, often abusive things you recognize in others are (or were at one time) also perceptible in us? We notice the wonderful and the not so great things. We embrace the lovely but retreat from the ugly. We do this because those same marvelous or appalling attributes have been (or still are) resident and lodging within our own being in some brilliant measure or shadowy degree. When we realize the intensity of our own shortcomings, we are more apt to receive and offer God's great grace to overlook or cover others' flaws. As soon as we sow grace and mercy toward ourself and others, we will reap great kindness and secure favor in our own life.

Our every thought needs to be seasoned with grace, mercy, love and wisdom in order to align ourselves with God's creative power, which overcomes every adversity.

When we forgive the hurtful things we observe in ourself and others, we are empowered to respond in the powerful love and forgiveness of Christ. If we retain a conscious awareness of any wrong we have suffered at the hands of another, we bind ourselves to them. However, if we choose to forgive them of all condemnation, prejudice and judgmental attitudes we have held toward them, we free ourself to ascend into a higher level of God consciousness. There is no condemnation for those who are in Christ Jesus. When we trust God with the outcome of everything in life, we can forgive and release everyone from the wrongs they have done. Do not worry about whether they get what they deserve!

A friend told me of a time she battled with letting go of the hurt and distress her husband's actions had caused her. She had attempted time and again to compel her husband to see the errors of his ways to no avail. She freely admits she just wanted him to reap for himself what he had sown. In anger, she finally professed to the Lord, "I will choose to forgive him out of obedience to you, but I refuse to let go and forget. If I do, he'll get off scot-free, and he may never completely understand the suffering I've had to endure because of his actions."

The Lord immediately replied to her simply with a whisper, "That is exactly what I have done for you." Completely undone and forever changed by God's loving revelation, my friend was freed from the binding cord of bitterness when she fully surrendered the desire to witness justice served by her own means.

Our every thought needs to be seasoned with grace, mercy, love and wisdom in order to align ourself with God's creative power, which overcomes every adversity. God is love. Therefore, the measure of power we possess is determined by the measure of love we house in our heart. Christ's indwelling presence will continually draw the lovely, beautiful and Christlike traits, people and angelic entities to us. We are moved to respect and love the positive people who exhibit the same marvelous attributes that are also present in our own life.

The imagination is a powerful, inspirational and creative energy. However, to the unbelieving person, the imagination is just the fancied, irrational notion of a bunch of unsound hallucinations full of erratic thought patterns. The unbelieving person thinks the imagination causes people to react to life as a suspicious victim who is controlled by false ideas and destructive mental concepts.

The negative, inappropriate use of the imagination produces fear, dread, doubt, unbelief and, quite frankly, a boring life of lack full of poverty, pain and disease. If one continues to maintain destructive thoughts, he or she will continue to reside in a pitiful, broken-down stronghold of poverty. That person will barely survive and will continually sustain a diseased state of existence. To those who lack imagination and hold fast to fear and all of these earthly, natural restraints, the expressions of Christ are not welcomed. *He* (the imagination working through the power of Christ) *was despised and rejected of men; a man of sorrows, and acquainted with grief* (Isaiah 53:3).

The Lord rewards us with creative vision that produces prosperity according to the measure of our righteousness or right standing in His likeness and image.

The Lord rewards us with creative vision that produces prosperity according to the measure of our righteousness or right standing in His likeness and image. The level of our compensation depends upon the cleanness of our hands and the childlike purity of our heart. *And you shall remember the*

Lord your God, for it is He who gives you power to (imagine how to create) *or get wealth, that He may establish His covenant, which He swore to your fathers, as it is this day* (Deuteronomy 8:18).

Those who embrace the power found in the mysteries of Christ dwelling within them always produce eternal fruit that remains. Believers become mentally fearless, stronger in their consciousness and wiser intellectually. They become prosperous in all of their ways.

The imaginative ones advance as leaders in business, equippers in ministry and inventors with intellectual acuity, governing their thoughts and actions by the laws of the creative, imaginative Spirit.

But we preach Christ crucified, to the Jews a stumbling block and to the Greeks foolishness, but to those who are called, both Jews and Greeks, Christ the power of God and the wisdom of God. Because the foolishness of God is wiser than men, and the weakness of God is stronger than men (1 Corinthians 1:23–25).

The level of one's success, joy and life achievements are dependent upon the energies he or she expels while searching for the divine knowledge of God. It is important to seek and discover the full dimensions of our personal gifts, passionate purposes and talents that we have not yet realized. The amount of prayerful effort we expend will decide how much of His will that we achieve on earth. Also consider that the types of thoughts on which we dwell govern the measure of weakness that we will tolerate. The beliefs we reflect to others and contemplate on will determine the degree of strength that we maintain.

The level of success, joy and one's life achievements is dependent upon the energies he or she expels while searching for the divine knowledge of God.

The pursuit of holiness (searching for the face of the invisible God) empowers the seeker of truth to take on a noble, godly character that continually increases in wisdom and understanding. An unselfish person who dwells on the mountain formed by pure thoughts will achieve the crown of accomplishing his or her heart's desire. *But the fruit of the Spirit is love, joy, peace, long-suffering, kindness, goodness, faithfulness, gentleness, self-control. Against such there is no law* (Galatians 5:22-23).

Believers' mastery of eating a well-balanced diet of the Fruits of the Spirit (love, joy, peace, gentleness goodness, kindness, patience, long-suffering and self-control) will cause them to continually rise to the top levels of social influence and power.

> *Truth conquers the darkness of ignorance by shining the light of change upon the path of those who choose to embrace a higher realm of thought.*

Spiritual elevations can only be maintained by keeping our eyes focused and centered on Christ. Christ is the power and wisdom of God. Therefore, we advance according to the measure of our understanding of the power of His mighty laws that are working within us. We are responsible for our own physical, mental and spiritual conditions.

But he who did not know, yet committed things deserving of stripes, shall be beaten with few. For everyone to whom much is given, from him much will be required; and to whom much has been committed, of him they will ask the more (Luke 12:48).

No matter how strong, supportive, bighearted or wise a person is, he or she cannot help the weak-minded, unimaginative person. People who are not receptive or teachable will break in illegally to steal whatever they want. The lazy person shouts, "You owe me!" They only put forth a minimal amount of effort. Therefore, they will only withdraw a small handout, just a fragment of what would have been available to them had they been diligent in their pursuits. The sluggard, in his ignorance, mistakenly thinks success happens to the lucky, the chance fortunate ones who happen to be in the right place at the right time.

The lethargic are blind to the years of diligent work and great faith that is developed in a person who has gone through difficult trials and gut-wrenching tests that build godly character. The reality is that a diligent lifetime of evolving has finally empowered that prosperous person to be among those who have chosen to excel and achieve success by overcoming the many struggles in life.

The amount of effort one sows in life will determine the amount of success they reap. No one receives anything from God that he or she has not worked for or earned through his or her labor of love and obedience to the Word. On the day of Pentecost, the Holy Spirit came upon those who fasted, prayed and waited on God in the Upper Room. The fire of His presence did not freely fall on everyone. It only consumed the chosen few who had set themselves apart to seek God with all their heart, and most of them were women.

The levels of spiritual inspiration, gifting, maturity and intellectual authority one possesses are directly related to the measure of the Fruits of the Spirit that are in operation in his or her life. The Fruits of the Spirit (another master key) exist in the higher level of our thoughts, so they can generate the degree of godly vision we follow and fulfill. The God you embrace, serve, worship and enthrone in your heart will determine the visions you see and the success you achieve in life.

> *True success comes when we dare to realize that we have accomplished the impossible dream through the power and wisdom of Christ.*

The weak-minded and poor (sick of body or emotionally troubled) remain oppressed, illegal aliens who are bound to negative self-concepts that hold them as captive slaves. They cannot experience freedom until they are willing to repent of their wrong doings and negative self-concepts. Their self-image must change. They have to decide to dream again. They must use their imagination in a positive, life-giving manner in order to reshape their destiny. The oppressed remain weak, subjected to and codependent upon the afflicting judgment of their oppressors.

Truth conquers the darkness of ignorance by shining the light of change upon the path of those who choose to embrace a higher realm of thought. Those who are diligent in their work ethic and dedicated to maintaining their higher thoughts and achieving their God-given purpose will continue to discover the favor of God's face shining upon them.

Productive people whose ambitions are big enough to dream the impossible dream and to make positive changes in the world will also challenge you to realize your own greatness. Imaginative leaders will always push you to reach your full potential. Be careful not to compare your measure of success to others', but do try to determine if you are using to the best of your ability all of the gifts, spiritual assets and talents God has given you. Do not hide your gifts, talents and abilities under a rock. The times when I have tried to dumb down or marginalize the extraordinary gifts God has given me in order to fit in have been the worst times in my life.

It is true that every man reaps the thoughts and impressions he has sown in his own heart (imagination). Life does not make mistakes. Man receives as his reward the things he does for himself and the things he does for others. The light of Christ shining in and through us awakens His positive, life-giving attributes in us.

So, keep your thoughts continually fixed on Christ; all that is authentic and real, honorable and admirable, beautiful and respectful, pure and holy, merciful and kind. And fasten the thoughts of your imagination on every glorious work of God, praising Him always (Philippians 4:8).

True success comes when we dare to realize that we have accomplished the impossible dream through the power and wisdom of Christ. By ascending the rungs of the beautiful, visionary ladder of integrity, we continue to obtain the ideal life that is formed by godly character. The imagination gives the Believer the power to behold a clear view of the truth of his or her destiny, for Christ is the Spirit of Truth. We are called to be true to the destiny God has given us.

Let Us Pray

Jesus, we ask that You empower us to overcome and defeat every enemy that has tried to form a weapon against us. Deliver us from all of the fear, doubt and unbelief that have caused us to spiral out of control. We renounce every failure. We choose to close the door on every trauma, and we reject all hurt. We are determined to be the answer to the problem and to provide kingdom solutions to others. We ask that the healing power of Your blood and Your virtue flow through us to cleanse and deliver us from all sickness, disease, poverty and any form of bitterness. Amen.

CHAPTER SEVENTEEN

Be Attitudes!

Now that we have learned that we become what our thoughts and attitudes project, allow me to close with Christ's intimate teaching to His disciples: the Beatitudes (*Be Attitudes!*) I have included an account of the proper posture we must maintain as a barometer and an encouragement so that you may reflect on your own present attitudes. Take a moment to review what Christ decreed, and prayerfully examine the imaginative thoughts and desires you currently hold about yourself and others in comparison. In order to fully step boldly into and maintain the new, we must be willing to shed any and all of the old.

> *One day, Jesus saw a vast crowd of people gathering to hear Him, so He went up the slope of a hill and sat down. With His followers and disciples spread over the hillside, Jesus began to teach them:*
>
> *"What spiritual prosperity and wealth is offered to you when you feel your spiritual poverty being void of arrogance, for there is no charge to enter the realm of heaven's kingdom. When you regard yourself as insignificant you are at the end of your rope there is less of you so there is more room for God. What delight comes to you when you peacefully wait upon the Lord! For you will find what your heart desires and long for.*

You're blessed and refreshed by God's grace even when you mourn over sin and repent, for you will be comforted when you feel that you have lost what you love, that which is the dearest to you. Only then can you truly let go to be embraced by the Holy One who is the dearest to you.

What blessing comes to you when you are spiritual secure, with a peaceful, gentle meekness of a kind heart and a sweet, loving spirit lives in you! For the self-controlled will inherit the earth.

You're blessed and joyfully nourished by God's goodness when you are content with just who you are—no more, no less. That's the moment you find yourselves confident owners of everything that can't be bought. How enriched you are when you actively seek right standing with God craving His righteousness! For in the fear of the Lord you will be surrounded and completely satisfied with fruitfulness. You're blessed when you've worked up a good appetite for God. He's heavenly food; bread, meat, manna and wine are the best meal you will ever eat.

How blessed, content and sheltered by God's promises you are when you demonstrate tender mercy! For tender mercy will be demonstrated to you. You're blessed when you care. At the moment of being care-full, you find yourselves cared for.

What bliss you experience when you anticipate and continually abide in God's presence. For when your heart is pure, full of integrity, moral courage and godly character then your eyes will be open to see more and more of God.

You're blessed when you are spiritually calm with a life full of joy in God's favor by getting your inside world—your mind and heart—put right at peace. Then you can see and express the character and power of God to the outside world as the Sons of God. How blessed you are when you make peace! For then you will be recognized as a true child of God. You're blessed when you can show people how to cooperate instead of fighting for a position by competing for a place of authority. That's when you discover who you really are and who you were created to be in your true place in God's Kingdom.

How enriched you are with God's inner peace and love, when you bear the wounds of being persecuted for doing what is morally right! For that is when you experience the realms of heaven's kingdom both now and forever.

You're blessed, morally courageous and spiritually alive with joy in God's goodness when your commitment to God provokes insults, false evil accusations, and persecution. The pain that you experience from persecution drives you even deeper into the depths of God's Kingdom. How ecstatic you can be when people insult and persecute you and speak all kinds of cruel lies about you because of your love for Jesus! So, leap for joy—since your heavenly reward is inexhaustibly great. For you are being rejected the same way the prophets were before you. Not only that—count yourselves blessed every time people put you down or throw you out or speak lies about you to discredit Me. What it means is that the truth is too close for comfort and they are uncomfortable. You can be glad and rejoice when that happens for though they don't like it, I do! And all of heaven applauds your life. Know that you are in good company. My prophets and witnesses have always gotten into this kind of trouble.

Salt and Light: Let me tell you the purpose of why you are here. Your lives are like salt among the people. You're here to be salt-seasoning that brings out the God-flavors of this earth. If you lose your saltiness, become bland, how can your 'saltiness' be restored? How will people taste godliness? Flavorless salt is good for nothing and will be thrown out and trampled on by others when their path is slippery. You've lost your usefulness and will end up in the garbage.

Here's another way to put it: You're here to be light, bringing out the brilliant rainbow God-colors in the world. God is not a secret to be kept. We're going public on the internet with this, as public and as noticeable as a city on a hill. Your lives light up the world. Let others see your light from a distance, for how can you hide a city that stands on a hilltop. I'm putting you on a light stand. You are the light of Christ to the world. Now that I've put you there on a hilltop, on a light stand—shine! Keep open house; be generous with your lives. Let your light shine before men in such a way that they may see your good deeds and moral excellence, to recognize and give honor and glory to your Father in heaven.

And who would light a lamp and then hide it in an obscure place? Instead, it's placed where everyone in the house can benefit from its light. If I make you light-bearers, you don't think I'm going to hide you under a bucket, do you? So, don't hide your light! Let it shine brightly before others, so that the commendable things that you do will shine as light upon them, and then they will give their praise to your Father in heaven. By opening up to others, you'll prompt people to open up with God, this generous Father in heaven" (Matthew 5:1–16).

Uniting our faith in the centrality of God's oneness makes everything that is possible for Him also possible for us when we function as joint heirs in Christ. Jesus Christ is the creative force that dwells within our imagination. *All things were made by Him* (Jesus)*; and without Him* (the imagination) *was not anything made that was made* (John 1:3).

He (Jesus) *was in the world, and the world was made through Him, and the world did not know Him* (imagination) (John 1:10).

The world does not recognize the beautiful light of Jesus. The world's eyes are still blinded by darkness. Unbelievers are captive to fear and doubt. They are dominated and blinded by the thoughts of failure, so they never see or take advantage of the myriad of opportunities that are presented right in front of them. Unbelievers become hopeless, quit and idly languish, living their lives parallelized by fear and aimlessly floating around in a hopeless pool of regret.

When the shining light of Christ's power within us becomes our focus, we can do All Things through Christ, whose joy strengthens us.

When the shining light of Christ's power within us becomes our focus, we can do All Things through Christ, whose joy strengthens us. For we know that nothing is impossible with God. God can do All Things! Anything that has been created began with an imaginative thought that sprang from a desire to reach the impossible.

Let's Pray

Dear Jesus, we know that nothing is impossible for You. We ask that You would unite us in the centrality of Your faith, making us one as You and Your Father are one. Help us to function as Your joint heirs so that Your creative force can be released through our imaginations. Amen.

Author's Note

Once we understand the importance of how and what we imagine, think and speak, we can shed the carnal mindset, and we can transition into believing, beholding, obtaining and maintaining our new identity. Volume IV offers divine revelation about the healing power of the subconscious, creative miracles and hindrances to having your prayers answered. You will learn how to release God's incredible and unlimited creative power through prayer and prophecy. Volume IV also presents valuable instruction of how to increase, advance and prosper as One New Man in this new era.

About the Author

DR. BARBIE L. BREATHITT

DR. BARBIE BREATHITT is a certified prophetic life coach (AskBarbie.com), published best-selling author, dedicated educator and experienced revelatory teacher of the divine, supernatural manifestations of God, whose greatest desire is to see other reach, fullfill and enjoy their destiny in God. She is recognized around the world as a leading master dream analyst (DreamsDecoder.com) and healing evangelist with deliverance, signs, wonders and creative miracles following. Barbie's prophetic seer gifting and deep spiritual insights have helped and equipped thousands of people, including business, media and government leaders, and ministries in over 40 nations understand God's mystical ways.

Dr. Barbie Breathitt teaches individuals, trains corporate professionals and business teams, government leaders and churches how to recognize, respond to and release the activity of God with unique strategies. Her sincere pursuit of God's Kingdom and His eternal truth make Barbie's Texas-based Breath of the Spirit Ministries, Inc. a predominant worldwide foundation.

An experienced teacher, published author, prophetic voice, dream analyst and healing evangelist, she has released God's love, presence and breath in prisons, hospitals, streets, Europe, third-world nations, television, radio and the internet. Her deepest desire is to see people fulfill their unique destiny here on earth. Barbie's training, resources and personal ministry help others to interpret and apply the direction God gives them through encounters, dreams and visions.

Barbie Breathitt personally learned and now passionately teaches God's Love, Presence and Breath. Her astute prophetic voice and accurate dream analyses have blessed those in prisons, hospitals, Europe and third-world nations, enabling many hungry people to grow. Barbie has abandoned herself to the Holy Spirit with miracles, signs and wonders following. Many individuals have been miraculously healed in her meetings while others have experienced the Presence of the Spirit as never before. Her infectious humor promotes unity with those inside and outside the church walls.

An ordained healing evangelist, Barbie has ministered for over thirty-five years around the world. Barbie established and conducted three prophetic training centers. Barbie now lives in Texas and opened Breath of the Spirit Center of Training in 2004. Breath of the Spirit offers a variety of courses on Healing, Revelatory Gifts, Dream Interpretation and Evangelistic Outreaches.

SPEAKING ENGAGEMENTS

Traveling around the world to share wisdom and insights regarding sound, biblical dream interpretation, Barbie is available for conferences, teaching and hands-on training. Please contact Barbie's ministry at Breath of the Spirit Ministries, Inc. through email (info@DreamsDecoder.com), the website (DreamsDecoder.com) or by phone at (972) 253-6653 for more information.

The *IMAGINE* Series

Volume I will help you understand and fully comprehend that the Spirit of Christ dwells mightily within your sanctified imagination. Discover how to supplant the carnal mindset that has limited God and the displaying of His grandeur in your life. By resting in and experiencing the presence and glory of God, you will be empowered to receive and harness His truth, divine wisdom, revelation and supernatural faith to confidently realize, embrace and achieve your unique purpose and grand destiny in this new era!

God has given you a riveting new identity in this new era! Volume II inspires and imparts how to further unlock and mature your imagination to fulfill God's purposes for your life. Discover what it is and how to shed your worldly, carnal self—how to transition into your higher IAM state of being in Christ. Advance beyond the limitations of the third dimension, and gain supernatural knowledge of the mysterious workings of the unrestrictive, four-dimensional realm of the Spirit.

The marvelous design and divine workings of the inspired imagination is further unveiled in this third volume. You will gain applicable spiritual understanding of how to access, unlock and interpret the meanings of visions and dreams that God skillfully fashions within your imagination. You will discover how to access your God-given authority. You will unite with the Fire of God to believe, see and prophesy in the NOW realm of God's faith. Through a broadened understanding of God's Word and clear spiritual insights into the profound power of imaginative prayer, you will be able to access the answers to your prayers that have been waiting on you to discover from the Genesis of creation. *IMAGINE* Volume III will equip and fully transition you into your new and glory-purposed identity in Christ. Your faith in God will explode into the supernatural faith of God!

In this instructive and illuminating volume, you will gain divine knowledge about the healing power of the subconscious, God's imaginative power and creative miracles. Volume IV will challenge what you believe, see and reason as truth and will help you identify the hindrances to having your prayers answered. God is restoring His people as One New Man! By using your sanctified imagination, you will discover how to come into agreement with God in order to effectively release your prophetic voice in this new era. You will obtain valuable instruction on how to increase, advance and prosper for God's kingdom purposes.

This fifth volume of the *IMAGINE* series brings the concepts learned in previous volumes full circle. Now that you have believed, beheld and obtained your new identity, you will discover the keys to successfully maintain that identity. You will encounter God's creative power, divine desire, godly disciplines of the imagination and lasting growth. The time to advance is NOW! Volume V delivers sound biblical teachings of how to use your creative imagination to release and prophesy into your God-ordained destiny and the destinies of nations. You will acquire the necessary knowledge and wisdom to effectively operate, persevere and prosper as a true Son of God and as One New Man.

DecodeMyDream.com

ONLINE DREAM JOURNAL

Barbie Breathitt is excited that so many people in God's Kingdom are exploring the understanding of dreams. Barbie's 30 years of study and experience in biblically-based, spirit-led dream interpretation are available in an online learning experience.

DreamsDecoder.com and DecodeMyDream.com are our interactive web sites, impacting dreamers all over the world. We believe it is vitally important to record God-given dreams and to search out the messages they contain. The site provides a free online dream journal, dream evaluations, dream mapping, prophetic analysis and comprehensive dream certification training.

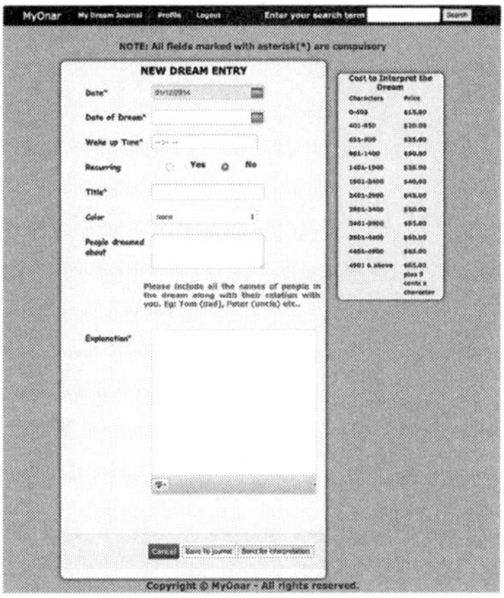

Sign up for your free online dream journal at DreamsDecoder.com. From the dream journal, you can easily submit your dreams for analysis by Barbie and our highly skilled dream analysts.

For additional resources by Dr. Barbie L. Breathitt, please visit
DreamsDecoder.com
Breath of the Spirit Ministries, Inc.
PO Box 1356 | Lake Dallas, TX 75065
(972) 253-6653

BOOKS

Dream Encounters–Seeing Your Destiny from God's Perspective is the "Rosetta Stone" to interpreting the illusive vapors of dreams. Uniquely inspired, and written to convince the greatest skeptics, and educate the most ardent believer, "Dream Encounters" will bring God's perspective, and understanding to the symbolic, visual, love letters, in the mysterious world of dreams. Take a journey into the sub–conscious night parables of the soul, to learn how dream truths impact your world; give direction, purpose, and destiny. Gain valuable keys to success by unlocking the mysteries of your dreams. Available as a paperback book, digital book or audio book.

Gateway to the Seer Realm: Look Again to See Beyond the Natural is written by Dr. Barbie Breathitt a gifted Seer who has years of personal experience interpreting dreams and ministering in the prophetic realm. You will gain valuable insights into understanding the ways of God and the divine supernatural realms of vision, dreams, angels, healing and destiny. Open new dimensions of revelation knowledge to learn how to access the Seer realm through intimate daily communication with God.

Dream Seer: Searching for the Face of the Invisible is written by Dr. Barbie L. Breathitt to help the reader understand the Seer Realms of angels, divine visions, the voice and presence of the Lord and dimensions where the ethereal vapors of our dreams will become substantial presences when we believe that anything is possible with God. God is the giver of dreams. Jesus is also the Redeemer. So, like a knight in shining armor, He comes to restore the dreams we have allowed to fall by the wayside. The Holy Spirit inspires us to recall the images He sent long ago. God has mapped out our future. He brings the events of the world to bear on our individual circumstances as He wills. When the events of our lives coincide with the correct timing of His plans, the next phase of our destiny ensues. The Holy Spirit knows the perfect time to bring the dreams and plans He has formulated to enable our purpose to come to pass.

There is only one right interpretation, God's. Every thing else is only shades of gray. Dream Interpreter will give you skill to correctly decipher the symbolism of your dreams. *Dream Interpreter* decodes symbols, types and shadows of images from a heavenly perspective in order to reveal the hidden mysteries that are contained within. Dream Interpreter will help the reader translate spiritual perceptions and happenings to accurately discern the events of the night. The gifted dream interpreter can decipher, convert and transform a concealed secret and then develop a blueprint for prosperity. You can learn to understand the evolution of vivid visions and dreams, the graphic picture language of nightmares and night terrors that come to visit and present truth about one's life. As a wise counsellor or life coach, dream interpreters fashion destiny bubbling up from the depths of the person's soul-potential to successfully guide the dreamer.

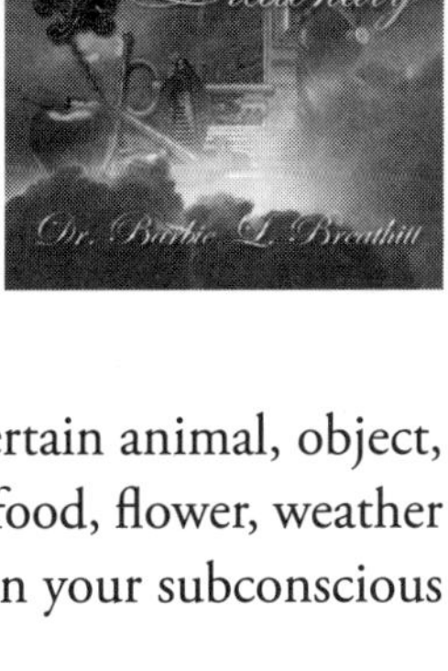

Acquiring a working knowledge of dream symbolism will enhance your ability to decipher the profound meanings of each symbol and then unlock the interpretation of every one of your dreams. Knowledge is power so learn to understand the mysteries that are hidden in your dreams. Their divine secrets will release your concealed potential so that you can design the destiny you have always longed for. Access the revelation knowledge stored in the pages of *A to Z Dream Symbology Dictionary*. Glean from ten thousand keywords and symbolic meanings that will inspire you to delve deeper into understanding why a certain animal, object, person, place, vehicle, article of clothing, tool, home, food, flower, weather pattern, action, emotion, color, or number appeared in your subconscious dream.

In her book, *Angels in God's Kingdom*, Dr. Barbie L. Breathitt propels readers beyond a natural understanding of the world around them to perceive and navigate the divine supernatural realms of the invisible world of angels. This one-of-a-kind comprehensive Biblical resource is full of progressive revelation and inspired spiritual truths. Dr. Barbie L. Breathitt covers fascinating topics detailing the origin, existence, and abode of angelic beings, their names, ministry functions, duties, and little known facts about the classifications of angels. She explores the nature of angels, the bold power of active faith and how the anointings of angels, seraphim, cherubim, heavenly creatures and host connect and guide us to and through the spirit world. Barbie shares her real life angelic encounters and the knowledge she has received through her diverse visitations, as well as her traumatic experience with the spirit of death. Discover the mystery of how recognizing the presence of powerful angels can redeem time when they are invited to step out of eternity to assist us in miracles, healing and deliverance. Learn how to prosper as the angels in God's Kingdom collide with the lawless evil forces of darkness and destruction. Gain spiritual understanding of how God's holy, intelligent angels clash with Satan's demons and diabolical fallen angels in today's modern world. Discover how the giants from the days of Noah are currently affecting society. And how we can defeat them through the blood of Jesus.

When Will My Dreams Come True? This handy booklet provides valuable detailed descriptions on dreams, visions and spiritual encounters. The information shared in these pages will educate the dreamer on the biblical techniques of dream interpretation. Through the study and application of the Hebrew alphabet and numbers, you will develop an Issachar anointing to discern the days, times and seasons of your dreams coming to pass. This collection of data research, priceless dream interpretation nuggets, gradient echelons of revelation, and prophetic vocabulary and terminology assembled in these pages will instruct dreamers on how to record and accurately interpret the meaning of their dreams, so they can pray, decree and declare them into being.

DREAM SYMBOL CARDS

These artistically designed dream symbol cards enable the dreamer to tap into the hidden meanings of the symbols that appear in many dreams and visions. These cards are also useful in helping the believer decipher the symbolic language that God uses to communicate through the revelatory realm of the Spirit. "God is speaking powerfully through dreams in this hour. So many believers are having significant dreams but do not always understand the significance of the symbols within them. Barbie Breathitt has done a marvellous job of preparing dream cards as a tremendous tool to help this process. They are very high quality and fully laminated for long-term use. I was impressed when I saw them." Patricia King XP Ministries (xpministries.com).

Acquire all of Barbie's artistically designed, laminated Dream Encounter Symbols Cards. They are available as single dream cards, in an excel spreadsheet or in spiral-bound collections.

Dream Encounters Symbols Volume I features the original 23 dream cards starter set with 1433 unique symbol definitions which makes an excellent gift for those who have a desire to learn the meanings of their dreams. The collection includes Animals, Apparel & Clothing, Body Parts, Color, Color and Music Healing, Creatures Great, Creatures Small, God's Dream Language, Going Places, Going More Places, Home Furnishings, Jewels, Musical Instruments, Numbers, People, Seers' Word of Knowledge Ministry Card, Spiritual, More Spiritual, Tools, U. S. State, Vehicles, and Weather and Natural Elements.

Dream Encounters Symbols Volume II has 18 different dream cards with 619 different symbol definitions. The collection includes Birds (4 dream symbol cards containing a myriad of positive and negative winged creatures), Bugs and Insects (3 cards), Money and Finance, Nutrition (5 cards outlining the meaning of different foods, sweets, meats and vegetables), Plants and Flowers (4 cards detail what different floral arrangements and bouquets represent. God is giving His Bride flowers in her dream. What is He saying to you?), and Varied contains a list of Frequent Dream Symbols.

Dream Encounters Symbols Volume III has an additional 29 spiral bound dream cards that combines 913 symbols complied in helpful categories for ease of study and use. The collection includes, Body Parts (an extensive compilation of 5 dream symbol cards), Building, Rooms & Structures (4 cards), People (12 individual cards listing careers, professions and callings), Spiritual & Military Weapons of War (4 dream symbol cards describing the spiritual weapons of prayer available to believers), and Vehicles (4 dream symbol cards boats, ships, trucks, cars, vans, airplanes, rockets and more).

Action Symbols Volume IV, has 13 artistically designed spiral bound dream symbol cards with 386 different movements such as flying, running, transporting, and translating actions.

Dream Sexology has 4 unique and informative dream symbol cards with 95 unique symbol definitions that explain the meanings of your intimate naked dream language.

Sports & Recreation Dream Symbols contains 13 dream symbol cards full of 321 different hobbies, sports, games and much more to help you take an active part in the game of life instead of sitting on the sidelines observing the excitement of others.

TEACHING SERIES

The Dream Encounter MP3 Downloads and Manual is designed to teach, train, activate, and impart the skills to interpret and understand how God communicates to us through dreams and visions of the night. Jesus continues to teach through night parables, in other words, inspired dreams. The Bible gives us three keys that will be used in the end-time revival and outpouring of the Holy Spirit. The course topics include: Dreams, Visions, Transportations, Translations, Lucid Dreams, Colors, Numbers, Dream Symbols, Dream Interpretation, and Dream Teams and Outreaches.

The Revelatory Encounter MP3 Downloads and Manual is a prophetic course designed to teach, train, activate, and impart the ability to hear God's voice for yourself and others. This training helps you recognize and remove hindrances to hearing God's still, small voice. The course topics include: Developing Godly Character and Integrity, Old and New Testament Prophets, False Prophets, Immature Prophets, God's Friends, Knowing God's Voice, Difference between the Gift of Prophecy and the Prophetic Office, Forms of Revelation, Four Categories of Prophecy, Spirit of Prophecy, Nine Gifts of the Holy Spirit, Interpretation, Application, The Seer, The Watchmen, Intercession, Prayer, Intimacy, Spiritual Authority, and Developing Prophetic Ministry Teams.

The Angelic Encounter MP3 downloads and Manual is a course that establishes a biblical foundation for the proof and ministry of angels. Topics include: What are Angels? Ministry of Angels; Types, Functions, and Characteristics of Angels; Satan and Fallen Angels; and Angels and the Death of the Saints. Barbie shares personal experiences of angelic visitations from her life.

The Healing Encounter MP3 Downloads and Manual is designed to teach, train, activate and impart the belief, skills and abilities to move in the healing ministry. Topics include: Introduction to Healing; Jesus, the Healer; Issues of the Heart; Four Aspects of Healing; The Faith Realm; Take Your Authority; You Get What You Expect; Miracles Today; Hindrances to Miracles; Suffering in Regards to Healing; God's Voice of Healing; You Must See it to Be it!; Keep Your Healing; Healing Scriptures; Baptism with the Holy Spirit; and Walking in the Healing Ministry.

OTHER RESOURCES

The Hand Prayer Points Chart is a reference card that matches illnesses and diseases with prayer points on the hand. Great for intercessors who need clear direction for their prayers.

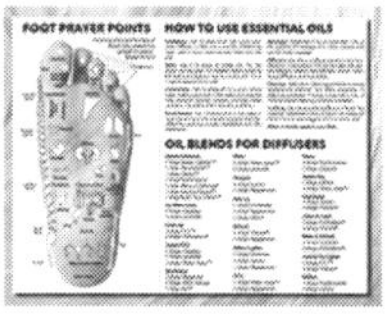

The Foot Prayer Points Chart is a reference card that matches the organs of the body, illnesses and diseases with prayer points on the foot. Great for intercessors who need clear direction for their prayers.

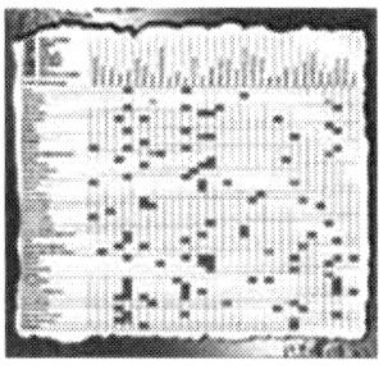

Healing Card is a reference card that matches illnesses and diseases with possible spiritual root causes. This Healing card is birthed from Barbie's ministry experiences and encounters of seasoned intercessors and those in healing ministries. Great for intercessors and individuals who need clear direction for their healing prayers.

Waking Words of Ancient Wisdom Make it a practice to notice the time on the digital clock as you awaken from a spiritually significant dream. The numbers displayed on the digital clock are often keys to help understand the message God is giving you in your dreams. Note the time on your clock, then look up the corresponding chapter and verse in the Bible. Allow the Holy Spirit to quicken the intended "Waking Words of Ancient Wisdom" to your heart and apply them in your life. This is a wonderful way to daily explore the Bible while you seek the deeper meanings of the treasures God is revealing to you through your dreams. Visit BarbieBreathitt.com to obtain detailed directions for use.

Dream Encounter Anointing Oil: Anoint yourself every night with this fragrant dream enhancing oil and pray for the Holy Spirit to visit you in your sleep. You will experience a heightened level of dreams, visions and visitations from the Spirit of God.

My Thoughts